STUDIES IN HISTORY, ECONOMICS AND PUBLIC LAW

Edited by the

FACULTY OF POLITICAL SCIENCE OF COLUMBIA UNIVERSITY

NUMBER 394

PARLIAMENTARY OPINION OF DELEGATED LEGISLATION

BY

CHIH-MAI CHEN

PARLIAMENTARY OPINION OF DELEGATED LEGISLATION

BY

CHIH-MAI CHEN, Ph.D.

NEW YORK
COLUMBIA UNIVERSITY PRESS
London: P. S. King & Son, Ltd.
1933

PRINTED IN THE UNITED STATES OF AMERICA

PREFACE

During the last few decades the delegation of legislative powers to the executive has proceeded at a rapid pace. The phenomenon has been common to all countries but it has been most marked and most discussed in England — the Mother of Parliamentary Government. Especially during the period which has followed the World War the attention of publicists and of the public has been directed to expounding and criticizing the practice in the light of the basic principles of the British constitution.

In the present monograph it is not my purpose to add to the already formidable literature which discusses the pros and cons of delegated legislation, and advocates measures of parliamentary and judicial control. My purpose is more modest—viz. to present the criticisms and defenses which were made in Parliament when statutes delegating legislative authority were being considered. Have the members of Parliament been jealous of their legislative power or have they consented, without serious objection, to successive abdications demanded by successive Governments? When Governments have urged delegations to the executive what grounds have they set forth to justify their proposals? What suggestions have been voiced in Parliament to the end that further delegations will be less necessary or that, if made, executive action will be more effectively scrutinized? The present monograph attempts to answer such questions.

The problem of course raises a number of so-called fundamental principles of the British constitution and naturally these principles have been enunciated in Parliament. When

I deal with this phase of the discussion I refer in footnotes to the literature which goes over the same ground and make no attempt here to thread the tortuous course through the distinctions and refinements of the writers of treatises. In the introduction I have summarized very briefly the opinions of certain writers. Judicial decisions on the problem have been thoroughly digested by Lord Hewart and Professor C. K. Allen and are therefore not considered here.

Of late, doubts have been raised as to the effectiveness of parliamentary discussions and of the influence exerted by parliamentary opinion. The critics have admired in contrast "the good old days" when eloquence and exuberant loquacity counted for something in the House of Commons and when (at least it was so believed) members changed their votes after listening to debates. Now, however, the increased rigidity of party ties, the greater control which party organizations exercise over their members, the greater dominance of the House of Commons by the cabinet, the increased complexity of legislation, and the greater importance of the press have combined to rob parliamentary debate of interest and effectiveness. Perorations and vituperations are less frequent than they used to be. The pages of *Hansard* are less lurid and more dull. The late Lord Balfour said that his idea of a distressing eternal punishment would be the enforced perusal of parliamentary debates.

It is to be expected, therefore, that parliamentary opinion on delegated legislation will not be exciting or very suggestive but a study of such opinion is well worth while. Since delegated legislation has rarely been a party issue it has formed the subject of debates which called forth genuine and candid convictions. The futility of these debates in forming majorities should not be allowed to lessen our interest in them as an index of British opinion and of parliamentary attitudes toward successive legislative abdications.

Like Mr. Phillotson's Roman-Britannic antiquities in Hardy's novel, the study of parliamentary opinion is a "comparatively unworked mine". As a rule English judges do not examine, in their interpretations of statutes, the discussions in the legislature which enacted them. Most of the writers on delegated legislation have been lawyers and it is thus natural that they have left parliamentary opinion out of their treatises. The present monograph, dealing almost exclusively with parliamentary opinion, is intended to fill this gap.

I had completed my work on the Debates in *Hansard* and the first draft of this manuscript had been written when there was published the *Report of the Committee on Ministers' Powers* (Cmd. 4060/1932). This Report, with the supporting memoranda and minutes of evidence, gives a comprehensive consideration of the whole problem of delegated legislation, with the exception of the aspect which I have examined—viz., parliamentary opinion: the criticisms made in the Houses of Parliament and the safeguards which have been suggested. My revision of the manuscript enabled me to incorporate a number of references to the Report and to its supporting volumes. Students of delegated legislation are under great obligations to the Committee for the care with which it analyzed the problem, formulated its recommendations and opened up such mines of information.

Finally, I wish to express my gratitude to Professor Lindsay Rogers, of Columbia University, under whose guidance and supervision this work was undertaken and completed. I am also grateful to Mr. Sanford Schwarz who has carefully gone over the manuscript with me and has helped put the book in its present form. Professors Robert L. Schuyler, Joseph P. Chamberlain and Arthur W. Mac-

Mahon, all of Columbia University, have read over the manuscript and have offered many valuable criticisms and suggestions which I have incorporated in the work.

C. M. C.

WASHINGTON, D. C., 1933.

TABLE OF CONTENTS

CHAPTER I

INTRODUCTION

The more fully the modern Parliament can be freed from the necessity of scrutinising narrowly the specific details of legislation, the more adequate is likely to be the performance of the functions for which it is, in fact, suited.

Harold J. Laski, *Democracy in Crisis* (1933), pp. 81-2.

IN continental countries it is an established practice to delegate extensive legislative powers to the executive government. Under the various French constitutions since that of the year VIII and the other European constitutions modelled on or suggested by those of France, "the executive government has, and freely exercises, an inherent power of making decrees, *réglements,* and similar orders and regulations which supplement the action of the legislature." [1]

[1] Sir Courtenay Ilbert, *Methods of Legislation* (London, 1912), p. 54. Sir Courtenay, in another book, said: "In Continental countries, as is well known, the delegation of legislative powers is far more extensively exercised than in England or in English-speaking countries. In France, statutes are often couched in general terms and enunciate a principle which the executive is to carry out in detail.... The regulations thus made are described in France as secondary legislation.... In Italy the power of the executive officials to make regulations is even more extensively used... the Government is practically allowed to suspend a law subject to responsibility to Parliament, and even to make temporary laws which are submitted to Parliament later. And Parliament uses very freely the power of delegating legislative power to the Ministers." *Legislative Methods and Forms* (London, 1901), p. 38. "In foreign countries", Professor A. V. Dicey wrote, "the legislature generally confines itself to laying down general principles of legislation, and leaves them with great advantage to the public to be supplemented by decrees or regulations which are the work of the executive." *Law of the Con-*

The theory of legislation is different in England and in English-speaking countries.[2] In these countries, legislative powers are supposed to be exercised by the legislature itself. Thus, in the United States, where the theory of separation of powers is most emphatically affirmed, Congress is always trying to regulate by bills matters of detail which in Continental countries are left to the executive.[3] In England, also, Parliament always prefers to reserve legislative powers exclusively to itself. As a result, English and American statutes have been burdened with elaborate detailed provisions and have attempted to provide beforehand, by precise statu-

stitution, 8th ed. (London, 1915), p. 49. For a recent description of the present method in France, see Edward McC. Sait, *Government and Politics of France* (New York, 1921), p. 46. Although English and American writers considered that these decrees and regulations issued by the French executive as acts of legislation, French writers were inclined to draw the distinction between "le pouvoir réglementaire" and "le pouvoir législatif", and insisted that "le réglement n'est pas la loi." A. Esmein, *Éléments de Droit Constitutionnel* (Paris, 1928), vol. ii, pp. 76-7. *Cf.* also Leon Duguit who said: "La doctrine et la jurisprudence admettant l'idée d'une distinction entre les matières dites législatives et les matières dites réglementaires, les premières ne pouvant etre réglementées que par une loi formelle et les secondes pouvant être réglementées par décrit. Mais cette distinction étant admise (et il est difficile de ne pas l'admettre) la difficulté devient très grande lorsqu'il faut déterminer quelles matières sont législatives, quelles réglementaires." *Manuel de Droit Constitutionnel* (Paris, 1907), p. 1031.

[2] "When an English or an American legislator drafts a statute," said President Lowell, "he tries to cover all questions that can possibly arise. He goes into details and describes minutely the operation of the Act, in order that every conceivable case may be expressly and distinctly provided for." *Governments and Parties in Continental Europe* (New York, 1896), vol. i, p. 44. If an Englishman, a Frenchman, and a German were given individually the task of drawing up a law with the same purpose to be accomplished, very different drafts would emerge, according to Professor L. Oppenheim. See his *The Future of International Law*, pp. 26-36, summarized in John P. Comer, *Legislative Functions of National Administrative Authorities* (New York, 1927), p. 11, note 2.

[3] Ilbert, *Methods of Legislation*, p. 49.

tory enactment, for every contingency which might reasonably be expected to arise.[4]

But, owing to various reasons to be presently stated, both England and the United States have found it increasingly difficult to maintain this so-called "legislative monopoly". With the problem in the United States we are not here concerned.[5] In the case of England, this "monopoly" is never complete.[6] Before the Glorious Revolution Parliament had been "delegating legislative powers in some matters, through the old prerogative machinery, by authorizing statutory Orders in Council."[7] After 1688, Parliament had also found it easy and convenient "to make use of the old machinery and to permit the statutory Order in Council to do what the prerogative Order in Council had been restrained from doing."[8] But from the early part of the eighteenth century to the early decades of the nineteenth century, this practice was gradually abandoned. The "legislative monopoly" grew insensibly. Even the war regulations of the French Revolutionary period were embodied in Acts of Parliament. Minute details of local application were to be found in the numerous Enclosure Acts. By about 1832, this "monopoly" began to relax. Powers to issue rules and regulations were more and more frequently delegated to the executive as the volume of social legislation gradually increased. The exigencies of the World War and its aftermath greatly accelerated the tendency. At the present time, many statutes, to use the metaphor of a writer in the *Times*,

[4] *Cf.* Dicey, *op. cit.*, p. 49, note 1.

[5] See Comer, *op. cit.*, and references there cited.

[6] *Cf.* Memorandum of Sir William Graham-Harrison, *Committee on Ministers' Powers: Minutes of Evidence*, vol. ii, pp. 33-5.

[7] Fairlie, J. A., *Administrative Procedure in Connection with Statutory Rules and Orders in Great Britain* (Urbana, 1927), p. 14.

[8] C. T. Carr, *Delegated Legislation* (Cambridge, 1921), p. 54.

"contain mere bones, and Government departments are given the power to supply any sort of flesh that they may think suitable." [9]

The words "Government Departments" used in these passages are important. When Parliament began to relax its "legislative monopoly" there had grown up in England a system of administrative departments which multiplied rapidly in number and which assumed greater and greater significance. The early delegations of legislative powers, as has been said, were made to the Crown in Council; later delegations were made in large part to these administrative departments.[10] Today the Order in Council system, though still used, has been more or less superseded by the departmental Order system, both in point of bulk and of importance.

The extent to which legislative powers have been delegated may be gauged from the number of Statutory Rules and Orders annually issued.[11] "More than half our modern

[9] Quoted in Sir J. Stamp, "Recent Tendencies Towards the Devolution of Legislative Functions to the Administration", *Journal of Public Administration*, vol. ii (1924), p. 32.

[10] Carr, *op. cit.*, p. 54.

[11] Mr. Carr, in his memorandum submitted to the Committee on Ministers' Powers, gives some figures to illustrate the extent of delegated legislation since 1894. These figures, which represent the number of Statutory Rules and Orders issued under various Acts of Parliament between 1894 and 1929 inclusive, are listed under three heads: Statutory Rules and Orders according to the definition of Section 3 of the Rules Publication Act of 1893, "General" Rules and Orders according to the definition of the "Treasury Regulations" of 1894, and the "Local" Rules and Orders according to the same definition. An analysis of these figures shows that between the years 1894 and 1929 inclusive, the average number of Statutory Rules and Orders per year was 1379. The average number between 1895 and 1905 inclusive was 1249.2 while that between 1906 and 1929 inclusive was 1708.2. Taking only the "General" Rules and Orders into account, however, the picture presented is totally different. The average number of "General" Rules and Orders issued between 1895 and 1905 inclusive is only 177.4, that between 1906 and 1920 inclusive increases to 895.2, while that between 1920 and 1929 inclusive

Acts are . . . incomplete statements of law." [12] The Statute Book does not contain all the laws of England. They must be sought also in the volumes of Statutory Rules and Orders published each year by the Stationery Office: and not all regulations are thus officially published.[13]

drops to 473.8. These figures cannot be taken too seriously because like all figures they serve more masters than one. But it is important to note the great increase in delegated legislation since 1906. After that date, the number issued in each year increased steadily until it reached 342 and 414 for the years 1912 and 1913 respectively. It is also important that, as Mr. Carr says, "the tide has now ebbed back to a pre-war mark", a phenomenon which he thinks gives evidence that the system is becoming stabilized. It is needless to cite the figures of the "Local" Rules and Orders. Suffice it to say that the annual figures for these Rules and Orders do not show a definite trend and that, with the exception of two war years, they have always outnumbered the "General" Rules and Orders sometimes by as many as ten times. *Committee on Ministers' Powers: Minutes of Evidence*, vol. ii, pp. 204 *et seq.* Mr. Hilton Young, in a written answer to a question put to him by Mr. Roberts, gives the figures of Statutory Rules and Orders of a public general nature as follows: 1890, 168; 1895, 222; 1900, 192; 1905, 185; 1910, 257 and 1913, 444.—144 H. C. Deb. 5 s. 429. These figures are slightly different from those given by Mr. Carr but the trend is the same.

[12] Carr, *op. cit.*, p. 1.

[13] The publication of these regulations is governed by the Rules Publication Act, 1893, and the "Publication Regulations" made under s. 3 (4) of the Act by the Treasury with the concurrence of the Lord Chancellor and the Speaker of the House of Commons.—For the "Publication Regulations", see *Statutory Rules and Orders Revised*, 1904, vol. xi, "Statutory Rules", p. 1. Before 1890, "though it had long been customary for Parliament to delegate to the Sovereign in Council or to some Government Department or public authority the power of making rules and orders for carrying out the provisions of statutes, there existed no systematic record of this delegated legislation. Much of it had been published in the London *Gazette*; other portions had appeared in Parliamentary Papers or Stationery Office publications; the remainder existed only in papers printed for the use of the departments concerned or was otherwise inaccessible, except so far as the rules might be found scattered over text-books or official manuals." Preface to *Index to Statutory Rules and Orders in Force on August 31, 1930*, p. iii. "For 1890 and each subsequent year an annual volume has been published" by the

Various writers have used various terms to describe the delegation of legislative powers to the executive authorities. Sir Courtenay Ilbert was the first one to use the term "delegated legislation" which has found wide acceptance.[14] The

Statute Law Committee and the Departments.—Preface to *Statutory Rules and Orders Revised*, 1919, p. v. The Rules Publication Act, 1893, and the "Treasury Regulations", 1894, defined the term "Statutory Rule" and the annual volumes since that of 1894 have been restricted to "Statutory Rules" so defined. The rules that were published were of a "public general character", excluding those "of a local, personal, or temporary character", which were sometimes indexed or listed. In 1896 was published the First Edition of *The Statutory Rules and Orders Revised*, containing in 8 volumes such Statutory Rules and Orders of a Public General character issued before 1890 (the first year covered by the series of Annual Volumes) as were then in force.... In 1904 there were published a new (the Second) Edition of 'The Statutory Rules and Orders Revised 1904' containing in 13 Volumes the text of such Statutory Rules and Orders of a Public General character as were in force on December 31, 1903.—Preface to *Index to the Statutory Rules and Orders*, 9th edition, 1919. These volumes were edited by Alexander Pulling, C. B. from 1890 to 1922 and by Cecil T. Carr, C. B. from 1922 down to the present time.

[14] Some other terms used are, for instance, "subordinate legislation", "subsidiary legislation", "demi-legislation", "sub-legislation", "administrative law", etc. The last mentioned term is most unhappy because it is commonly used as an equivalent for the *droit administratif* of Continental law. *Cf.* Sir John Marriott's use of the term, 226 H. C. Deb. 5 s. 2511.

Delegated legislation must be sharply distinguished from the delegation of judicial or quasi-judicial powers to the executive or to special administrative tribunals. With the delegation of judicial or quasi-judicial powers we are not here concerned but as its relation with delegated legislation is seldom pointed out in treatises on the subjects, a digression seems proper. Recent statutes delegating legislative powers frequently grant to the executive the power to decide disputes arising under such statutes or under the regulations issued in pursuance of them. While the ordinary law courts have no supervisory power over the rules and regulations issued by the executive it is well settled that the validity of such rules and regulations may be examined by them when the question is raised in the course of a suit between a complaining individual and the executive on the plea of *ultra vires*. The transfer of the jurisdiction

term " may mean either exercise by a subordinate authority, such as a Minister, of the legislative power delegated to him by Parliament; or the subsidiary laws themselves, passed by Ministers in the shape of Departmental regulations and other statutory rules and orders." [15] As used in this work it means none of these, but rather the *practice* of delegating legislative powers, by Act of Parliament, to the executive authorities.

The chief characteristic of the English practice of delegating legislative powers is its lack of system. Legislative powers are delegated " as and when the need arose in Parliament ", [16] " to amend, extend, vary, repeal, apply, commence,

to decide disputes arising under such statutes and involving the regulations issued by the executive from the courts to administrative tribunals deprives the courts to that extent of their power of independent scrutiny. Some statutes, moreover, empower the executive to issue regulations for the purpose of setting up administrative tribunals or for the purpose of providing these tribunals with rules of procedure. In the view of many writers, this delegation of both legislative and judicial or quasi-judicial powers to the executive violates some of the fundamental guarantees of the Constitution and increases enormously the powers of the Government at the expense of Parliament and the courts of law. Moreover, the increase of the powers of the Government means an increase in the powers of the bureaucrat, of whose wisdom and discretion Englishmen exhibit a temperamental distrust and skepticism. The ouster of the courts means, in the phrase of the Webbs, that the bureaucracy has now entrenched itself against interference. The resentment and fear evoked by the increased authority of Downing Street and Whitehall cause the delegations of legislative and judicial or quasi-judicial functions to be sharply challenged and subjected to criticism and attack.

[15] *Report of the Committee on Ministers' Powers*, Cmd. 4060/1932, p. 15. Mr. Carr thus defines delegated legislation: " When the King in Parliament, our supreme law-making authority, expressly allows some other authority to undertake this kind of supplementary law-making, the result is what we call 'delegated legislation' ". Carr, *op. cit.*, pp. 1-2. When Mr. Carr talks about the " result " as being delegated legislation, he is using the term in the second sense given by the Committee on Ministers' Powers.

[16] *Report of the Committee on Ministers' Powers*, Cmd. 4060/1932, p. 16.

or terminate Acts of Parliament."[17] In general, these powers fall into three categories: direct amendment of the statutes, creation of legislative machinery affecting the commencement, duration or application of a statute, and power to make regulations which elaborate, supplement or help to work out some principles laid down by Parliament.[18] The powers delegated may be exercised in two forms: by means of the Order in Council or by means of the Departmental Order. The former system was much used formerly but it has now been more or less superseded by the latter method.[19]

Three forms of safeguards are generally provided. The "administrative safeguard" is that provided by the Rules Publication Act, 1893, and the "Publication Regulations" issued thereunder. The "parliamentary safeguard" is generally embodied in the empowering statutes themselves, requiring the regulations issued thereunder to be laid before Parliament. Some regulations cannot take effect until they are confirmed by a resolution.[20] Others must be laid before

[17] Sir Lynden Macassay, "Law-Making by Government Departments", *Journal of Comparative Legislation and International Law*, vol. v. (1923).

[18] Carr, *op. cit.*, ch. ii.

[19] *Report of the Committee on Ministers' Powers*, Cmd. 4060/1932, pp. 26 *et seq.* A Provisional Order is not delegated legislation because it "requires confirmation by an Act of Parliament to give it the force of law." *Ibid.*, p. 25. "Provisional Orders... do not involve any true delegation of legislative power, because they derive their validity, not from the act of the department, but from the statute by which they are confirmed; and they are included among Acts of Parliament, and not the statutory orders of the year." Lowell, *op. cit.*, vol. i, pp. 364-5. *Cf.* Sir Courtenay Ilbert, *The Mechanics of Law-Making* (New York, 1914), pp. 139 *et seq.*

[20] A list of the cases in which an affirmative resolution is now required will be found in the *Index to the Statutes in Force* under the heading "Parliament" reprinted in *Committee on Ministers' Powers: Minutes of Evidence*, vol. ii, p. 36. It should be noted that while this class of regulations are confirmed by a resolution the Provisional Orders are confirmed by an Act of Parliament.

Parliament for a defined period of time, ranging from 20 to 100 days.

These are of two distinct classes. Those of the first class do not take effect until they have been so submitted for a prescribed period, and do not become Statutory Rules until that period has expired. Those of the second class take immediate effect and become Statutory Rules at once: in some cases the Rules of this second class are subject to annulment on resolution of either House within a fixed time, but without prejudice to their interim operation.[21]

The " parliamentary safeguard " is reinforced by a " judicial safeguard ". It is a principle of English law " that any power conferred upon a Government department by statute must be exercised in strict conformity with the terms of the statute, and that any action by such department which is not so exercised should be treated by a court of law as invalid ",[22] at the instance of a third party, on the plea of *ultra vires*.[23] In this fashion, the courts of law are enabled to examine the regulations issued by the executive and to declare them null and void when they are found to exceed the authority conferred. Various provisions of modern statutes have, however, seriously restricted this power of " independent scrutiny ". For one thing, some of the clauses in recent Acts are so loosely drafted that the courts often find it difficult to determine the intent of Parliament.[24] Again, some

[21] Preface to the *Index to Statutory Rules and Orders* (1919), 9th ed., p. vi. For a detailed classification of the various forms which the " parliamentary safeguard " now assumes, see Carr, *op. cit.*, p. 41 and *Report of the Committee on Ministers' Powers*, Cmd. 4060/1932, pp. 41-42.

[22] Professor A. V. Dicey thinks that the case of *Board of Education* v. *Rice* (1911), A. C. 179 "establishes, or rather illustrates in its application to particular circumstances " this principle. " The Development of Administrative Law ", *Law Quarterly Review*, April, 1915.

[23] F. J. Port, *Administrative Law* (London, 1929), p. 147.

[24] *Report of the Committee on Ministers' Powers*, Cmd. 4060/1932, p. 38.

Bills provide that regulations issued in persuance of the authority conferred thereby "shall have effect as if enacted in this Act" or "shall have effect as if they were contained in this Act".[25] This provision has been much discussed, and criticized, on the assumption that it prevents a court of law from inquiring into the regulations.[26]

Professor F. J. Port takes an extreme view of the present alleged ineffectiveness of the judicial safeguard when he writes:[27]

> Where the Order cannot be made unless both Houses by resolution approve the draft, an appeal to the Courts against an Order so made would obviously be in the nature of an attempted interference with parliamentary functions. Nor would such an appeal be any more effective where an Order is laid before both Houses for 21 or 28 days, and can during that period be annulled by a resolution of either House. Negatively, Parliament has approved it. From the point of view of appeal on the ground of *ultra vires,* therefore, the only class of delegation which gives an appellant a sporting chance is that in which the language of the statute is reasonably restricted in scope and where submission to Parliament is not required.

The view of Professor Port is challenged by Lord Chief Justice Hewart. He writes:[28]

[25] The legal effect of such provisions was considered in *Institute of Patent Agents* v. *Lockwood* (1894), A. C. 347; *Chester* v. *Bateson* (1920) 1. K. B. 829; *Newcastle Breweries* v. *The King* (1920) 1. K. B. 854; and *Minister of Health* v. *The King (on the Prosecution of Yaffé)* (1931) A. C. 494.

[26] *Report of the Committee on Ministers' Powers,* Cmd. 4060/1932, p. 40. Professor C. K. Allen thinks that the case of *Institute of Patent Agents* v. *Lockwood* (1894) A. C. 347 which deals with a Clause of this nature in the Patents, Designs and Trade Marks Act, 1883 (s. 101 (3)), "has laid it down once for all that the effect of this provision is to place the departmental order entirely beyond the scrutiny of the courts." *Bureaucracy Triumphant* (London, 1931), p. 76.

[27] *Op. cit.*, p. 151.

[28] Hewart, *The New Despotism* (New York, 1929), p. 96. In his

The first sentence in this passage ignores the dicta of Younger, L. J., (as he then was) in '*R. v. Electricity Commissioners*' (1924) 1 K. B. at p. 212, and the word 'obviously' is therefore not justified, even though it be assumed that the Court has no jurisdiction in such a case to quash the Order as *ultra vires*. As for the rest of the passage, there is certainly no authority in support of the views expressed, and they appear to be entirely erroneous.

So much for a brief discussion of the safeguards. Upon the effectiveness of each we do not here venture any conclusion. On a later occasion we will briefly summarize the opinions of some of the writers on this subject.[29] The essential difference between the parliamentary and the judicial safeguards is, of course, that the courts can never do more than prevent the executive from acting illegally.[30] Only

memorandum submitted to the Committee on Ministers' Powers, Sir William Graham-Harrison, the present First Parliamentary Counsel, states the present position of the judicial safeguard most clearly when he divides it into the following aspects: "(a) The delegated power must be exercised in accordance with the provisions of the relevant enactments with respect to procedure, the form and substance of the rules and the sanction, if any, and the rules are invalid if the conditions precedent to the exercise of the power are not complied with. (b) Rules are only valid in so far as they do not contradict the Statute under which they are made or the general law, or they must be construed so as not to contradict it. (c) The Rules must be necessary for carrying out the purpose of the Act and will be held *ultra vires* where they cannot on any reasonable construction be held to fall within the objects of the relevant Statute. (d) A direction that Rules are to be laid before Parliament is directory only, that is to say, in such cases the Rules come into operation when made and their operation is not suspended until they are laid. (e) Where Rules are to be laid, the court has no power, as it has in the case of bye-laws, to inquire into the reasonableness of the Rule providing it is *intra vires*." *Committee on Ministers' Powers: Minutes of Evidence*, vol. ii, p. 37.

[29] See *infra*, pp. 28 *et seq.*

[30] Herman Finer, *The Theory and Practice of Modern Government* (London, 1932), vol. ii, p. 1474.

Parliament has the power to require the government departments to act reasonably.[81]

The increasing predilection of Parliament for delegating legislative powers has aroused considerable discussion both within and without Parliament.[82] It seems proper, there-

[81] Hewart, *op. cit.*, p. 64.

[82] It may be of interest to discuss briefly the literature on delegated legislation. Earlier writers on English political institutions do not consider the practice in the light of some of the recent writers. They are, on the whole, in favor of the practice and consider it as a convenient method to solve some of the legislative problems of Parliament. They do not look upon it as a violation of the principles of the English constitution as some later writers do. For instance, Alpheus Todd, writing in 1867, saw the necessity of entrusting to public departments and other executive bodies certain subordinate legislative powers.—*On Parliamentary Government in England* (London, 1867-9), vol. i, pp. 291-2. The second edition of this work, edited by his son from the notes of the author, contains a chapter bearing the significant title of " Legislation by Public Departments ".—(London, 1887), ch. ix, pp. 470 *et seq.* This is probably the earliest comprehensive treatment of the subject. It gives evidence of the remarkable foresight of the author who deals with a problem which was becoming increasingly important but which was neglected by his contemporary writers. Similar tribute must be paid to Professor F. W. Maitland who, in 1886, realized that "year by year the subordinate government of England is becoming more and more important. The new movement set in with the Reform Bill of 1832: it has gone far already and assuredly it will go farther.... The constitution does not now-a-days consist merely of King and Parliament, privy council, courts of law and some purely executive officers, such as sheriffs, obeying their commands. We have changed all that since the first Reform Act. The governmental powers, the subordinate legislative powers of the great officers ... have become of the greatest importance, and to leave them out of the picture is to make the picture a partial one-sided obsolete sketch." *Constitutional History of England* (Cambridge, 1920), pp. 501, 506. Professor A. V. Dicey, in his classical work *Law of the Constitution*, does not describe the practice of delegated legislation in England but he advocates the adoption in England of the Continental method of legislation so that Parliament would be enabled to deal effectively with general legislative principles. (London, 1920), 8th ed., pp. 49-50. This opinion of Professor Dicey is especially interesting when we remember that many arguments against the Continental method of legislation are based upon the theories advanced by Dicey himself. Three

fore, by way of preface to our analysis of parliamentary

of Sir Courtenay Ilbert's books discuss the problem briefly. It is Sir Courtenay's contention that Englishmen will find it difficult to subscribe to the suggestion of Dicey. *Legislative Methods and Forms* (London, 1901), pp. 36-42; *Methods of Legislation* (London, 1912), pp. 54 *et seq.* and *The Mechanics of Law-Making* (New York, 1914), pp. 139 *et seq.* President Lowell and Sir William Anson, writing at about the same time, allotted only limited space to the subject.—*The Government of England* (New York), rev. ed. (1916), vol. i, pp. 363-6; *Law and Custom of the Constitution* (London), Gwyer, ed. (1922), vol. i, pp. 316 *et seq.* Readers of the latter work should also consult its earlier editions because Sir Maurice Gwyer, who edited the latest edition, is a strong advocate of delegated legislation and has written his ideas on the practice into the work. Cecil T. Carr's *Delegated Legislation*, though short, is perhaps the first book which deals exclusively with the subject. By reason of his editorship of the annual volumes of *Statutory Rules and Orders*, Mr. Carr's account and suggestions are entitled to high respect.—(Cambridge, 1921).

In 1929, Lord Hewart, the Lord Chief Justice of England, "left the Bench to break a lance for the pristine purity of Dicey's Rule of Law", as Professor Felix Frankfurter says, and set forth in his *The New Despotism* a series of violent charges against what he terms "the encroaching power of the bureaucracy".—(London, 1929), (New York, 1929). This book more or less focused the attention of the British public on this problem of ministerial and bureaucratic encroachments in the form of delegated legislation and the delegation of judicial or quasi-judicial powers. Professor William A. Robson, a year before, published his *Justice and Administrative Law* (London, 1928) in which he advocated the institution in England of a system of administrative courts. These two books came at a time when Parliament was making its most vigorous attack upon delegated legislation during the debate on the Local Government Act, 1929. Mention should also be made of a series of articles written by Professor C. K. Allen which appeared in the *Quarterly Review* and which was later collected in a book entitled *Bureaucracy Triumphant* (London, 1931). These discussions of the practice of delegated legislation and "administrative law" brought the issue before the public in such a way that the Lord Chancellor (Lord Sankey) had to allay concern by the appointment, on October 30, 1929, of an authoritative and learned committee of inquiry called the Committee on Ministers' Powers. This Committee, headed by Lord Donoughmore and later by Sir Leslie Scott, held fifty-four sittings at twenty-two of which oral evidence was taken. It submitted a report in 1932, supplemented by two companion volumes. Together, they form the most up-to-date and authoritative account of the whole system of delegated legislation and judicial or quasi-judicial decisions. (For other literature, see *Bibliography*.)

opinion to summarize briefly the views of some of the writers upon the subject. To many writers, delegated legislation is a tendency "impossible to avoid".[33] "In the working of constitutional government," Alpheus Todd found in 1867, "experience has proved that certain subordinate powers of legislation must be entrusted to almost every leading department of state."[34] Mr. Gladstone, in his address to the electors of Greenwich on January 23, 1874, remarked:[35]

> The duties of Parliament have reached a point where they seem, for the present, to defy all efforts to overtake them. I think we ought not only to admit, but to welcome, every improvement in the organisation of local and subordinate authority which, under the unquestioned control of Parliament, would tend to lighten its labours and to expedite public business.

Lord Thring, the first holder of the office of First Parliamentary Counsel, wrote in 1877 that "the adoption of the system of confining the attention of Parliament to material provisions only, and leaving details to be settled departmentally, is probably the only mode in which Parliamentary government can, as respects its legislative functions, be satisfactorily carried on."[36]

The causes of delegated legislation are found in the social and political changes which took place in England during the past hundred years. These changes have enormously enlarged and complicated the functions of the state. Whereas formerly its main functions were defense and police, the state

[33] H. Hilton Young, "The Authority of the House of Commons", *Contemporary Review*, July, 1925.

[34] Todd, *op. cit.*, 1st ed., vol. i, p. 291.

[35] *London Times*, January 24, 1874, p. 8, quoted in Todd, *op. cit.*, 2nd ed., vol. i, p. 478.

[36] *Practical Legislation* (1877 ed.), p. 12 (1902 ed.), p. 44, quoted by Sir William Graham-Harrison in *Committee on Ministers' Powers: Minutes of Evidence*, vol. ii, p. 33.

has now assumed the duties of "doctor, nurse, schoolmaster, trader, manufacturer, insurance organiser, house builder, town planner, sanitary engineer, railway controller, and . . . a hundred other capacities."[37] The discharge of these additional functions of the state calls for more legislation. The "busy workshop" at Westminster not only becomes busier than ever but is literally crushed by the weight of its legislative business. Parliament is "overwhelmed by the multiplicity of its normal duties."[38] The limited time at its disposal is decidedly not enough for Parliament to scrutinize intelligently the lengthy and complicated Bills with all the details which in modern Bills are so abundant.[39] Many important clauses are passed without adequate discussion or with none at all.[40] Often, the Bills involve technical matters

[37] William A. Robson, "A Charge of Despotism", *Contemporary Review,* January, 1930. *Cf.* H. J. Laski, "The Growth of Administrative Discretion", *Journal of Public Administration* (1923), p. 92.

[38] Sidney Low, *The Governance of England* (New York, 1920), 2nd ed., p. 291.

[39] The length of modern Acts is proverbial. For example, the National Insurance Act, 1911, comprises 115 Sections and 9 Schedules, occupying, in all, 112 pages of Chitty's *Annual Statutes.* The Local Government Act, 1929, is made up of 138 Sections and 12 Schedules, taking 182 pages of the same collection. It might be of interest to note that since 1832 the number of Public General Acts passed in each year has steadily decreased. Between 1832 and 1870, the average number of Acts passed is 113.1. The average for the years 1871-1920 drops to 59.1; for 1921-1929, 58; for 1930, 44. Professor C. K. Allen argues that the decrease in the number of Acts passed proves that the contention that Parliament is congested is unfounded. He evidently forgets the enormous increase of regulations in recent years which greatly relieves Parliament and the increased length of the statutes. See Allen, *Bureaucracy Triumphant,* pp. 145-6. A list of the number of statutes passed between 1800 and 1923 is given in Wan Hsuan Chiao, *Devolution in Great Britain* (New York, 1926), pp. 108 *et seq.*

[40] "Parliament", says Professor Herman Finer, "is cruelly congested; there is insufficient time for all the work, legislative, administrative, and financial, to be so much as undertaken; that which is undertaken

which require careful and protracted consideration by experts and specialists. The members of Parliament frequently lack the aptitude to comprehend and deal with these matters.[41] To be sure experts may be summoned. But the process of summoning experts and of hearing testimony in the committee rooms upstairs wastes a great deal of time and is difficult, if not totally impracticable, in an unwieldly body such as the Committee of the Whole to which most important Bills are now referred. Those members who are experts along certain lines would, in all probability, welcome any opportunity to offer their knowledge to the House, but, the question of time aside, they often fail " to catch the Speaker's eye ". Circumstances and difficulties such as these have given rise to the practice of delegating subordinate legislative powers to the executive. Parliament has no other alternative. " The truth is that if Parliament were not willing to delegate law-making power, Parliament would be unable to

is gabbled through in the midst of general inattention and too often absenteeism; the various forms of closure shut off debate; the Standing Committees so pre-empt the attention of members of Parliament that they vote on the resolutions of the Chamber in entire ignorance of the issues. . . ." "Special Report from the Select Committee on Public Business ", *Political Quarterly,* July-Sept., 1932.

[41] Sir Maurice Gwyer writes: "The trend of modern legislation and the limited amount of time at the disposal of Parliament make the practice [of delegated legislation] inevitable. Modern legislation concerns itself so closely with the life of the individual citizen, and touches him at so many points, that in the case of many Acts it would in practice be impossible for Parliament to deal itself with the mass of detail implicit in their provisions." *Committee on Ministers' Powers: Minutes of Evidence,* vol. ii, p. 3. Sir William Graham-Harrison writes: "It would be impossible to produce the amount and the kind of legislation which Parliament desires to pass, and which the people of this country are supposed to want, if it became necessary to insert in the Acts of Parliament themselves any considerable portion of what is now left to delegated legislation." *Committee on Ministers' Powers: Minutes of Evidence,* vol. ii, p. 35.

pass the kind and quantity of legislation which modern public opinion requires." [42]

Modern Bills, besides being lengthy and technical, often involve principles and policies hotly disputed by hostile sections of public opinion. With the widening of the social basis of the House of Commons, it has ceased to be "socially homogeneous" and can no longer be regarded as "the best club in Europe". Party lines are sharply drawn upon issues which the parties in truth and at bottom dispute. Opposition becomes increasingly uncharitable and persistent. "Speakers increased in number and speeches in length." [43] Members of the Opposition seize upon every minor matter to discredit and criticize the Government. In order that these minor matters may be exempted from party strife, it is thought proper to leave them for the government departments and other public authorities to regulate by administrative regulations.

The meeting of unforeseen contingencies and crises, according to Mr. Carr, "is the greatest justification for delegated legislation".[44] It is practically impossible for the legislative draftsmen to foresee and thus to provide for all the possible contingencies that attend the daily application of the statutes. Some power to cope with these contingencies as they arise must therefore be allowed the executive.[45]

[42] *Report of the Committee on Ministers' Powers*, Cmd. 4060/1932, p. 23.

[43] Carr, *op. cit.*, p. 15.

[44] *Ibid.*, p. 21. Professor Allen admits that "emergency legislation, if an evil, was a necessary evil" although he laments that "sometimes it went much farther than even emergency demanded." *Bureaucracy Triumphant*, p. 10. *Cf.* Port, *Administrative Law*, pp. 137-8.

[45] "It is quite impossible," say Wade and Phillips, "at the time of the initial legislation in Parliament to foresee all the conditions that may arise out of the measure that is being considered. It is, therefore, necessary to give to an administrative authority power to deal with the situation by means of rules and regulations." *Constitutional Law*, p. 91-2.

National crises, such as wars or strikes or epidemics, demand rapid decision and quick action. Delay may result in a calamity which despatch may easily avert. Parliament is not always in session and its procedure is dilatory and cumbrous. Emergency situations must be handled with efficiency and an executive authority with wide discretionary powers is decidedly better fitted to meet the situations than a parliamentary mob.

These facts—parliamentary congestion, the complicated and technical nature of modern statutes, the intensification of party strife in the House of Commons, and the demand for efficiency in times of crisis—combine to make delegated legislation "an inevitable concomitant of modern legislation." [46] Its inevitability is, with few exceptions, generally admitted by writers on the subject. Differences of opinion, however, exist upon the question whether the practice is a desirable one or not.

One group of writers considers the practice quite desirable. Carr is perhaps the strongest defender of this form of law-making. Delegated legislation, according to him, is an "invaluable administrative device".[47] It is not inconsistent with the principle of parliamentary supremacy. On the contrary, "each successive delegation . . . has been a fresh recognition of that supremacy." [48] Far from reviving the old controversy between the Crown and Parliament, "the successive delegations by Parliament . . . are victories at the expense of the Crown".[49] The fact that powers were delegated by Parliament and not exercised by the Crown itself "was a proof, not of weakness, but of strength." [50]

[46] Sir Maurice Gwyer, "The Legislative Functions of Government Departments", *Journal of Public Administration*, vol. iii (1930).

[47] Carr, *op. cit.*, p. 56.

[48] *Ibid.*, p. 48. [49] *Ibid.*

[50] *Report of the Committee on Ministers' Powers*, Cmd. 4060/1932, p. 138.

Under "the constitutional control of Parliament," Mr. Alpheus Todd found that [51]

> there is an undeniable advantage in the practice itself. The proper limits within which such powers may be exercised having been prescribed by statute with directions that all such minor or provisional legislation shall be duly submitted to Parliament,—either for *tacit* approval or direct ratification,—it is often expedient to entrust the settlement of details of practical legislation, requiring special or local knowledge, to the public departments immediately concerned therein. By this means the benefit of local experience is obtained in the determination of such questions, and especially where the consent of parties interested has been freely given,—Parliament is relieved from the consideration of matters which may be troublesome to decide, without infringing upon local interests.

"Statutory rules," wrote Sir Henry Jenkyns in 1893,[52]

> are in themselves of great public advantage because the details which are the subject of them can thus be regulated after a Bill passes into an Act with greater care and minuteness, and with better adaptation to local or other special circumstances, than they possibly can be in the passage of the Bill through Parliament. Besides they mitigate the inelasticity which would often otherwise make an Act unworkable, and susceptible of modifications from time to time by the Government departments at any time of the year as circumstances arise.

What was true when Mr. Todd and Sir Henry Jenkyns wrote

[51] *On Parliamentary Government in England* (London, 1887), 2nd ed., vol. i, p. 470.

[52] Quoted by Carr in *Committee on Ministers' Powers: Minutes of Evidence,* vol. ii, p. 204. *Cf.* Sir Edward Troup who says: "This delegation has the twofold advantage that the rules can be made after such expert inquiry and full hearing of objectors as is impossible in ordinary parliamentary procedure, and that rules can be modified to meet new conditions or to defeat evasions more easily and quickly than by the passing of amending acts of parliament." *The Home Office* (London, 1925), p. 251.

is still true today. " Parliament ", in the opinion of Miss Ellen Wilkinson,[53]

> can only deal really effectively with the principles and general plan of proposed legislation. The details should be left to the experts. This would make it possible for the House of Commons to discuss thoroughly and intelligently the broad outlines and enable a more real control over the Executive to be exercised than can possibly be the case when Parliament becomes an obstacle race, the sole duty of the Opposition being to provide the hedges and ditches on the course.

" The practice, again, permits of experiment being made and thus affords an opportunity, otherwise difficult to ensure, of utilising the lessons of experience." [54] Sir William Graham-Harrison, the First Parliamentary Counsel, in his memorandum submitted to the Committee on Ministers' Powers, emphasized [55]

> the superiority in form which, as a result of the different circumstances and conditions under which they are respectively prepared and completed delegated legislation has over Statutes. In most cases the time available for drafting Bills is inadequate and their final form when they have passed both Houses is generally unsatisfactory. On the other hand, Statutory Rules can be prepared in comparative leisure and the subject matter can be arranged in a logical and intelligible shape uncontrolled by the exigencies of Parliamentary procedure and the necessity for that compression which every Minister (however much in debate he may use the draftsman as a whipping-boy) invariably requires in the case of a Bill.

Coming from the First Parliamentary Counsel, this passage

[53] Miss Wilkinson in *Report of the Committee on Ministers' Powers*, Cmd. 4060/1932, p. 138.

[54] *Ibid.*, p. 52.

[55] *Committee on Ministers' Powers: Minutes of Evidence*, vol. ii, p. 35.

ought to carry a weight commensurate with the authority and experience which his office naturally gives him.

One of the chief objections to delegated legislation is that many of the rules and orders issued by the executive, though generally officially published according to the provisions of the Rules Publication Act, 1893, escape notice by the public. Even this phenomenon has its advantage in certain respects, such as in the field of the issuance of bank notes by the Bank of England where a rule or an order enjoys a definite advantage over an Act of Parliament because the psychological effect produced by a rule or an order is much less than an Act passed under the full flare of publicity and under the constant fire of criticism.[56]

[56] "Prior to 1914 the only way by which the Bank of England in times of crisis could increase its fiduciary issue was through the suspension of the Bank Act by Parliament, and it was therefore open to the Government of the day to lay down its requirements as to the rate of discount as a condition precedent to the application to Parliament. By the Currency and Bank Notes Act, 1914, the Bank of England and the Scotch and Irish Banks of Issue were permitted to issue notes in excess of the limit laid down by laws so far as this might be authorised by the Treasury, and subject to any condition attached to that authority. The Committee on Currency and Foreign Exchanges after the War (Cunliffe Committee) in their first report recommended the continuance of this arrangement, subject to the qualification that it should be obligatory to inform Parliament at once by means of a Treasury minute laid before both Houses of any action taken. This gives Parliament an opportunity for discussion, and though the increase in the fiduciary issue will already be a *fait accompli*, it must be remembered that even with the pre-war system the emergency conditions which necessitated the suspension of the Bank Act might call for immediate action on the part of the Government in advance of the approval of Parliament. The difference in the machinery is therefore less than might appear at first sight, but the two methods may have different effects on the attitude of the Bank and of the public. It might be suggested that the efforts to avoid any increase in the fiduciary issue would possibly be less strenuous if it can be authorised by an executive department as a part of a recognised procedure than if the sanction of the Legislature to the suspension of an Act of Parliament were required. This would be obviously a disadvantage. On the other hand, if the increase in the fiduciary issue can be authorised by the

On the other hand, there is a group of writers who see in delegated legislation a mischievous practice which must be strictly circumscribed if not abolished. Delegated legislation, it is said, violates the principle of separation of powers. "It is the task of Parliament to make the laws, and the real business of the Executive is to govern the country in accordance with the laws which Parliament has made . . . it is . . . dangerous to hand over to the Executive the power of making laws as well." [57] It follows from this that when legislative powers are exercised not only by Parliament but also by the executive, the principle of parliamentary sovereignty goes by the board.[58] Furthermore, the practice might lead to excessive powers in the executive. Since Bills are now largely drafted in the Government departments and forced through Parliament under the pressure of Government whips, "the Cabinet is therefore in a position through its members at the head of a Government Department to embark on a particular policy which has never in any detail been discussed in Parliament or communicated to the public." [59]

The method of "skeleton legislation" is objectionable in many respects.

"(1) It will result in hasty legislation;

"(2) It will tend to deprive members of Parliament of their sense of responsibility;

Executive, the situation may be deprived of the catastrophic appearance that is inevitably associated with the temporary suspension of an Act of Parliament, and the psychological effects of this difference in atmosphere may be of genuine practical importance." C. H. Kisch and W. A. Elkin, *Central Banks.* (London, 1928), pp. 94-6.

[57] Hewart, *op. cit.*, p. 77.

[58] J. A. R. Marriott, *English Political Institutions,* 3rd ed. (Oxford, 1925), p. xxxiv.

[59] Macassey, "Law-making by Government Departments," *Journal of Comparative Legislation and International Law* (1923), p. 73.

"(3) It will place the subject at the mercy of officials of the Central and Local Authorities;

"(4) It will make it very difficult for the true state of the law to be ascertained even by lawyers." [60]

Finally, the practice of delegated legislation has gone too far, much farther than is necessary. Emergency laws, such as D. O. R. A., have done violence to most, if not all, of the basic principles of the Constitution.[61] Many other provisions delegating legislative powers, such as "the power to remove difficulties" clause or the "as if enacted in this Act" clause, are in many cases unjustified. The practice has, in fact, been abused, and "it is the abuse of the system that calls for criticisms." [62]

The opinions of Professor Dicey are unique among writ-

[60] Memorandum of Mr. H. A. Hill, representing the Property Owners' Protection Association, *Committee on Ministers' Powers: Minutes of Evidence*, vol. ii, pp. 70-1.

[61] Of the phenomena exhibited during the four years of warfare, none is more remarkable than the docility with which the people of this country submitted to the abrogation of many of their most cherished rights. Restrictions which must have been a torment to the restless spirits of Hampden and Wilkes, and even led the more ancient shades of King John's barons to contemplate another expedition to Runnymede, were received and obeyed almost without question. Such fundamental principles of the Constitution as those expressed by the phrases Government by Parliament, the Responsibility of the Executive to the Legislature, the Liberty of the Subject, Trial by Jury, Open Law Courts, Freedom of Speech, the Freedom of the Press, and An Englishman's House is his Castle, were attacked, whittled down, and in some cases reduced to mere shreds of their former consequence. What Dicey calls the essential characteristic of the British Constitution, namely 'the absence of arbitrary power on the part of the Crown, of the Executive, and of every other Authority in England', went into retirement, and the old, long-unused Prerogative was exalted as it had not been since the days of Charles I and Strafford." Sidney W. Clarke, "The Rule of Dora", *Journal of Comparative Legislation and International Law*, 3rd series, vol. i (1919).

[62] Hewart, *op. cit.*, p. 85.

ers on delegated legislation. After stating the practice on the Continent of Europe, he said:[63]

The cumbersomeness and prolixity of English statute law is due in no small measure to futile endeavours of Parliament to work out the details of large legislative changes. This evil has become so apparent that in modern times Acts of Parliament constantly contain provisions empowering the Privy Council, the judges, or some other body, to make rules under the Act for the determination of details which cannot be settled by Parliament. But this is only *an awkward mitigation of an acknowledged evil, and the substance no less than the form of the law would, it is probable, be a good deal improved if the executive government of England could, like that of France, by means of decrees, ordinances, or proclamations having the force of law, work out the detailed application of the general principles embodied in the Acts of the legislature.* In this, as in some other instances, restrictions wisely placed by our forefathers on the growth of royal power are at the present day the cause of unnecessary restraints on the action of the executive government.

[63] *Law of the Constitution*, 8th ed., pp. 49-50. Italics mine. Sir Courtenay Ilbert commented on this passage of Professor Dicey as follows: "The ordinary Englishman, as represented by the average member of Parliament, would find much difficulty in assenting to the proposition laid down by an eminent author" (Professor Dicey). "If his liberty of action is to be subjected to restraint, he prefers that the restraint should be imposed by laws which have been made after public discussion in a representative assembly. He will readily admit that the application of a different principle is in accordance with the habits and traditions of Continental countries, and is necessary in countries like India, but he dislikes its application at home. Therefore, although he acknowledges the impossibility of providing for every detail in an Act of Parliament, and the consequent necessity of leaving minor matters to be regulated by statutory rules or by executive discretion, he scrutinizes with a jealous eye provisions which delegate the power to make such rules, or which leave room for the exercise of such discretion, and insists that they should be carefully expressed and limited, and be hedged round with due safeguards against abuse." *Legislative Methods and Forms*, pp. 39-40.

As said above, whether the writers regard delegated legislation as a desirable tendency or not, all of them recognize that it is inevitable. The problem then, as one writer puts it, is [64]

> how Parliament may delegate sufficiently to relieve itself of detail, and at the same time may retain so much supervision over the exercise of the delegated powers as will ensure not merely that they are not abused, but that their freedom from abuse is apparent to all men.

Delegated legislation, in other words, must be "kept within due limits and accompanied by due safeguards." [65] What are "due limits" and "due safeguards"?

Many writers think that the various forms of safeguards are quite sufficient to prevent the executive from abusing the delegated powers. The Rules Publication Act, 1893, though generally admitted to be sadly restricted in operation and badly needing revision, is effective because Government departments are as a rule extremely loath to disregard its requirements and thus to expose themselves to public criticism. Moreover, in the making of regulations, the departments are almost without exception under the continuous scrutiny of powerful associations and bodies representing interests that are affected by these regulations.[66] The "Parliamentary safeguard", these writers think, is likewise effective in ensuring the close surveillance of Parliament over regulations issued by the executive. "The plan whereby either House may present an address praying for annulment has worked

[64] Sir Hugh Orange, "Legislation by Witehall", *Nineteenth Century*, June, 1932.

[65] Ilbert, *op. cit.*, p. 41.

[66] Memorandum of Sir Arthur Robinson and E. J. Maude, representing the Ministry of Health, submitted to the Committee on Ministers' Powers. *Committee on Ministers' Powers: Minutes of Evidence*, vol. ii, p. 120.

well in practice and provides a real safeguard "[67] because " when powerful interests are antagonized by the exercise of rule-making powers the procedure by way of address is effective."[68] Again, the " judicial safeguard " will effectively discourage the Government departments from exceeding their powers[69] and will also nullify any regulation that is *ultra vires.*[70] Finally, rule-making powers are delegated to Ministers who are responsible to the House of Commons.[71] The whole system of delegation is in fact built upon the theory of ministerial responsibility and any criticism of the practice is a criticism of the whole system of cabinet or parliamentary government.[72]

The views of these writers are sharply challenged by others. Many writers regard the " administrative safeguard " as quite ineffective because of the limited operation of the Rules Publication Act.[73] The " parliamentary safeguard," moreover, is, in their opinion, a mere illusion. The mass of regulations that are laid before Parliament are not scrutinized by Parliament as they manifestly should be. " Parliament never discusses them. It is nobody's business to call Parliament's attention to them: No committee is ever appointed to review them, and no parliamentary time is allo-

[67] Memorandum of Sir Maurice Gwyer. *Committee on Ministers' Powers: Minutes of Evidence,* vol. ii, p. 6. See also Sir William Anson, *Law and Custom of the Constitution,* Gwyer ed. (London, 1922), vol. i, pp. 318-9.

[68] Memorandum of Robinson and Maude, *op. cit.*, p. 123.

[69] Even Lord Hewart admits this point. " The liability to annulment may," he writes, " have the effect of making the legislating department somewhat more careful than it would otherwise be." *The New Despotism*, p. 90.

[70] See *supra*, pp. 19-20.

[71] Gwyer Memorandum, *op. cit.*, p. 4.

[72] *Ibid.*, p. 1.

[73] Rules Publication Act, 1893, Section 1. Hewart, *op. cit.*, p. 88.

cated for discussing them." [74] "Usually the matter goes by default." [75] Lord Hewart, moreover, finds "that much the larger number of statutory rules and orders are not required to be submitted to Parliament at all" and that "in the great majority of such statutes [delegating power] there is no provision for Parliamentary control of any sort." [76] The provisions in some statutes, are so ill-defined and loosely drafted that in the opinion of some writers, they "have the effect of employing the sovereignty of Parliament to oust the jurisdiction of the Courts." [77] Thus, the judicial safeguard is said to have faltered. Finally, the responsibility of the Min-

[74] Muir, *How Britain is Governed*, p. 61. It should be pointed out that motions for an address annulling a regulation are classified by the Standing Orders as "exempted business" and can be brought by any member after 11 o'clock. The difficulty is that a good House to debate the motion is hard to secure at that hour.

[75] Port, *op. cit.*, p. 355. *Cf.* also C. K. Allen, *Law in the Making*, p. 326, and A. Lawrence Lowell, *The Government of England*, vol. i, p. 365. I have investigated the *Journals of the House of Commons* and the *Parliamentary Debates* since 1890 and found that during these forty years, a total of 51 motions for an address praying for the annulment of a regulation were moved. Among them, 31 were negatived, 11 carried, 8 withdrawn and 1 "discharged." It is interesting to note that during the War, no motion of this sort was moved and that only 2 motions were carried after the War, the last instance being in 1925. These motions, whether carried or negatived or withdrawn, were usually accompanied by extensive debates. The regulations that were questioned in early years generally concerned education or the administration of charities while the regulations discussed after the War were issued under various Insurance, Local Government, and other Acts. This comparative infrequency of motions for annulment, if the number of regulations issued and laid before Parliament be considered, may be viewed from various angles. By the critics of delegated legislation, it may be adduced as evidence of the ineffectiveness of this form of safeguard. On the other hand, the champions of delegated legislation may take it as a proof of the excellence of the regulations that the Government departments had issued. In truth the evidence is too scant to justify either view.

[76] Hewart, *op. cit.*, p. 95.

[77] Hewart, *op. cit.*, p. 77.

isters to Parliament does not give Parliament a real and effective control over the legislative acts of the executive. Professor Dicey has discounted the effectiveness of this safeguard.[78] Lord Hewart shares his opinion: [79]

What with the collective responsibility of Ministers, and the inexorable demands of the party system, once the mischief has been done, the whole force of the Parliamentary majority tends to be directed, not so much to undoing it, as to preventing a defeat in a Parliamentary division. 'This is our lobby', say the Whips, when the critical moment comes, and at the eleventh hour the private member is naturally disposed to acquiesce.

Various suggestions have been made to better the safeguards or to set up new ones. Those suggested by members of Parliament are treated in a later chapter. Those suggested by the writers and by the Committee on Ministers' Powers may be here summarized: [80]

(1) They favor a clearer definition of the law-making powers delegated by Parliament by

(a) more careful drafting of the enabling statutes,[81]
(b) more careful drafting of rules and regulations,[82]

[82] *Ibid.*, p. 70.

[78] "The Development of Administrative Law in England", *Law Quarterly Review*, April, 1915.

[79] Hewart, *op. cit.*, p. 12.

[80] The recommendations of the Committee on Ministers' Powers, fifteen in number, have been widely commented upon in the press. Many reviews, most of them listed in the bibliography of this monograph, have been written. In the Houses of Parliament, many questions have been addressed to the Government asking them what measures will be taken to put these recommendations into effect. See, for instance, 262 H. C. Deb. 5 s. 551; 265 H. C. Deb. 5 s. 1716-7; 266 H. C. Deb. 5 s. 359; 1772; and 270 H. C. Deb. 5 s. 506. Up to the end of 1932, no action has been taken by the Government.

[81] *Report of the Committee on Ministers' Powers*, Cmd. 4060/1932, p. 65.

(c) appending to proposed enabling statutes and rules and regulations explanatory memoranda for the information of Parliament and the public; [83]

(2) They favor the standardization of the terms used in statutes to describe the instruments by which law-making power conferred on Ministers by Parliament is exercised; [84]

(3) They favor maximum publicity and consultation with affected interests whenever practicable; [85]

(4) They favor the standardization of the procedure for laying rules and regulations before Parliament; [86]

(5) They favor the abandonment of the so-called " Henry VIII Clause " in all but the most exceptional cases and the strict limitation of the scope and time of the clause in such exceptional cases; [87]

(6) They favor the abandonment of clauses which are designed to exclude the jurisdiction of the courts to enquire into the legality of a regulation or order in all but the most exceptional cases and the strict limitation of the scope and time of the clauses in such exceptional cases; [88]

(7) They favor the revision of the Rules Publication Act, 1893, along lines that will make its field of operation more comprehensive and more definite; [89]

(8) They favor the creation of a joint committee of both Houses or a committee in the House of Commons to scrutin-

[83] *Ibid.*, pp. 66, 67.

[84] *Ibid.*, p. 64.

[85] *Ibid.*, p. 66; Carr, *op. cit.*, p. 36; Hewart, *op. cit.*, p. 154.

[86] *Report of the Committee on Ministers' Powers*, Cmd. 4060/1932, p. 67.

[87] *Ibid.*, p. 65.

[88] *Ibid.*, p. 65.

[89] *Ibid.*, p. 66; Hewart, *op. cit.*, p. 155. *Cf.* Carr's suggestion in *Committee on Ministers' Powers: Minutes of Evidence*, vol. ii, pp. 209-210.

ize and report on proposed enabling statutes or rules and regulations laid before the Houses;[90] and

(9) They favor the strengthening of the judicial safeguard.[91]

These are, in general, the suggestions and recommendations made by the Committee on Ministers' Powers and the writers on delegated legislation. Many of a more specific nature cannot be here listed. Mention should, however, be made of the desire on the part of some writers to enlist the cooperation of the press in trying to give delegated legislation as much publicity as is practicable.[92] "The problem which the critics raise is essentially one of devising the best safeguards."[93] But what is best only the angels may tell.

[90] *Report of the Committee on Ministers' Powers,* Cmd. 4060/1932, p. 67; Hewart, *op. cit.,* p. 153. Wade and Phillips, *Constitutional Law,* pp. 93-4.

[91] The lawyers are particularly jealous for the powers of the courts of law. The case against delegated legislation built up by Lord Hewart and Professor C. K. Allen centers around the problem of the control of the courts. Similar ideas are expressed by Sir Lynden Macassey in the *Journal of Comparative Legislation and International Law,* vol. v, (1923) and Sir Leslie Scott, in *Contemporary Review,* May, 1931. *Cf.* also *Report of the Committee on Ministers' Powers,* Cmd. 4060/1932, p. 65.

[92] Mr. C. T. Carr and Lord Hewart are among those who favor the co-operation of the press. Carr, *op. cit.,* p. 36 and Hewart, *op. cit.,* p. 154.

[93] *Report of the Committee on Ministers' Powers,* Cmd. 4060/1932, p. 54.

CHAPTER II

A Brief Historical Sketch of Parliamentary Opinion of Delegated Legislation

In England, more than elsewhere, constitutional progress has been the result of social development.

J. R. Green, *A Short History of the English People*, preface to the first edition.

Into the history of delegated legislation it is needless to probe; admirable and lucid accounts have been furnished us by a number of hands.[1] No writer, however, has discussed the opinions expressed by members of Parliament when Bills for the delegation of legislative powers to the Privy Council, the Government departments and other executive bodies were presented to Parliament. The history of these opinions this chapter will present.

First, there are a few general considerations to be stated. Not all Bills delegating legislative powers are of equal interest to the members of Parliament. Consolidation Bills, though often of great importance, are not generally debated at length. The subjects of some Bills may be of slight interest to the members while those of other Bills may affect the rights and obligations of their constituents and thus be of grave concern to them. The time allotted by Parliament to the discussion of Bills varies with the subject-matter of the Bills presented and the interest of the mem-

[1] Historical accounts of delegated legislation may be found in C. T. Carr, *Delegated Legislation* (Cambridge, 1921), ch. vi; F. J. Port, *Administrative Law* (London, 1929), ch. ii; *Committee on Ministers' Powers: Minutes of Evidence*, vol. ii, pp. 33 *et seq.* (Memorandum of Sir William Graham-Harrison).

bers therein. The length of the discussion upon delegated legislation in the debates on particular Bills is thus not indicative of the attention given by Parliament to delegated legislation. In other words, the question of delegated legislation may be hotly argued in the debate on one Bill although the length to which the Government have gone in demanding legislative powers may not in that case be nearly as drastic as in another Bill on which practically no debate occurs.

Closure, it must be recalled, was introduced into British parliamentary practice in 1880. The average length of debates in the House of Commons is thus different in the periods preceding and following the adoption of the closure, and no comparison can be made of the length of debates during the two periods. In the House of Lords, however, the situation is different, for closure is not there applied.

Though not strictly a vital issue in politics, delegated legislation often forms the subject of partisan debates. In their persistent effort to discredit and overthrow the Government in power, members of the opposition have frequently seized upon delegated legislation as a weapon of attack. John Morley once said that much of parliamentary debate is dispute between men who in truth and at bottom agree, but invent arguments to disguise and contrive a difference. Opposition to delegated legislation may be just one of these invented arguments.

I have chosen the year 1832 as the starting point of this narrative. It goes without saying that the history of a haphazard and unsystematic subject such as delegated legislation does not lend itself to division into well-defined periods. The year 1832, however, ushered into English history a new order of things of which delegated legislation is but one important result. The first Reform Bill, which put the House of Commons on a wider and more democratic basis, inaugurated an era of active political and social reform.

As the legislative activities of the House of Commons multiplied, most of the conditions which gave rise to the delegation of legislative powers began to appear. " The new movement ", as Professor Maitland noted, " set in with the Reform Bill of 1832." [2]

Our first period starts with 1832 and terminates with 1906. Though many important political and social reforms were enacted during this period, individualism and *laissez faire* still dominated mid-Victorian thought. The domination of these doctrines was continued because of the series of Tory Governments and the exigencies of the South African War. The period of large-scale collectivist legislation did not begin until after 1906 when the Liberals were returned with an overwhelming majority in Parliament. Many and extensive powers were delegated to the Government departments and minor executive authorities. The year 1906, thus, can serve as a convenient, if somewhat arbitrary, landmark in our survey.

Many of the Bills passed between 1832 and 1906 delegating legislative powers were enthusiastically received by Parliament. The " great and extraordinary " and " very arbitrary powers " delegated to the Privy Council by the Prevention of Cholera Act, 1832, for the prevention of the epidemic and for the care of the afflicted were granted by Parliament with enthusiasm. Lord Althorp, the Minister in charge, thought that " the exigency of the case . . . was such as to justify it in the eyes of all rational men." [3] One member declared that " all the powers which were necessary ought to be given " [4] while another asked the Privy Council to " consider themselves fully authorised to act even

[2] *Constitutional History* (London, 1920), p. 501. *Cf.* Port, *op. cit.*, p. 138.

[3] 10 *Hansard*, 3 s. 337-338.

[4] 10 *Hansard*, 3 s. 342.

before the bill passed through Parliament."[5] Sir Robert Peel

suspected no abuse of the powers which it was proposed to confer, and therefore thought it better to give a discretionary power to the Privy Council than for Parliament to attempt to define the precise nature of the measures to be adopted.[6]

The Destructive Insects and Pest Act, 1877, which delegated powers to the Privy Council to arrest the spread of the "Colorado beetle" was received with general approval by both Houses of Parliament.[7]

Many of the Clauses which delegated legislative powers during this period were received and passed by Parliament without adverse criticism or attack. Thus, Section 3 of the County and District Constabulary Act, 1839, which gave important rule-making powers to "one of Her Majesty's Principal Secretaries of State," was not attacked at all.[8] The comparatively long debate on the Metropolitan Police Act, 1839, contained only one or two scattered comments on the investment of the magistrates with rule-making powers.[9] The Commons Enclosure Act, 1845, and the Charitable Trusts Acts, 1853, both delegating powers to make Provisional Orders, were not debated in either House of Parliament.[10] The clauses authorizing the issue of Orders in Council in the Naval and Marine Pay and Pensions Act, 1865, failed to provoke any attack. Although Section 47 of the Endowed Schools Act, 1869, was said to have given to the Commissioners "despotic" and "arbitrary" powers,[11]

[5] 10 *Hansard*, 3 s. 270.

[6] 10 *Hansard*, 3 s. 339.

[7] See *Hanard*, 3 s., vol. 236 for the debate.

[8] See *Hansard*, 3 s., vol. 50 for the debate.

[9] 49 *Hansard*, 3 s. 113.

[10] See *Hansard*, 3 s., vol. 82 for the debates.

[11] 194 *Hansard*, 3 s. 1396 and 1411.

this grant was not questioned after the Government reminded Parliament of the fact that the exercise of these powers by the Government was founded upon the theory of ministerial responsibility and that Parliament had the power to challenge and to supervise their exercise.[12] Section 23 of the Municipal Corporations Act, 1882, conferred wide powers on the Municipal Councils to make by-laws subject to the disallowance of the Privy Council. An amendment to require the explicit approval by the Privy Council of the by-laws before they came into effect was withdrawn when the Government declared it "unnecessary."[13] The delegation of legislative powers by the Patents, Designs, and Trade Marks Act, 1883, evoked no protest whatever in the Houses. On the contrary, one member "hoped that the power conferred on the Board of Trade would be actively exercised."[14] The Ancient Monuments Act, 1882, contained a Schedule which listed the ancient monuments to be protected. A private member moved that the Crown-in-Council should be authorized to enlarge the list by Order, a motion which was readily accepted by the Government.[15]

The extensive "power of the Local Government Board

[12] 194 *Hansard*, 3 s. 1371 and 1410. In this debate, Mr. Gladstone, the Prime Minister, commenting on the proposal that the names of the Commissioners should be included in the Bill instead of appointed by the executive, said: "Whenever the Government were made responsible for the acts of the Commissioners the practice of Parliament was not to desire them to be named in the Bill. On the other hand, if they were named in the Bill the effect was to throw a great deal of the responsibility upon the House of Commons. Now, all the acts of the Commissioners would be null and void, unless approved by the Privy Council, and the responsibility for their recommendations was that of the Government. The course taken by the Government was in accordance both with precedent and reason." 196 *Hansard*, 3 s. 1747.

[13] 269 *Hansard*, 3 s. 209-210.

[14] 278 *Hansard*, 3 s. 370.

[15] 273 *Hansard*, 3 s. 1599, 1849-1850.

to remedy defects" delegated by Section 108 of the Local Government Act, 1888, (the Henry VIII Clause) was not attacked at all. Parliament thus agreed to the delegation of a power to "amend" the principal Act without any protest. The other powers delegated by various clauses were likewise granted without any severe criticism. On the contrary, one member of the Opposition even moved an amendment substituting the Order-in-Council system for the Provisional Order system provided in the Bill.[16] Section 24 of the Railway and Canal Traffic Act, 1888, which was said to have wrought "a peaceful revolution",[17] was only mildly criticized by Parliament.[18] One member even saw the "ad-

[16] The clause "Power to remedy defects" empowered the Local Government Board, according to Lord Hewart, "to make such orders as appeared to them necessary for bringing the Act into operation, and by any such order to modify the provisions of that or any other Act of Parliament, so far as might appear to the Board necessary for that purpose." *The New Despotism* (New York, 1929), pp. 245-6. The clause has subsequently appeared in ten Acts, a list of which appears in *Report of the Committee on Ministers' Powers*, Cmd. 4060/1932, pp. 123 *et seq.*, the most recent being Section 130 of the Local Government Act, 1929. Of late years much of the discussion on delegated legislation has turned about this power possessed by some of the Ministers and Government departments. See, for instance, the memoranda submitted to and the questions asked by the Committee on Ministers' Powers. *Committee on Ministers' Powers: Minutes of Evidence*, vol. ii, consult index under "power to make Orders to remove difficulties". See also Sir Hugh Orange, "Legislation by Whitehall", *Nineteenth Century*, June, 1932. This clause has been dubbed "the Henry VIII Clause" because of its supposed resemblance to the Statute of Proclamations passed during the reign of Henry VIII in 1539, which provided that the King, with the advice of His Council, could under certain circumstances issue proclamations which should have the force of an Act of Parliament. But, according to the Committee on Ministers' Powers, this comparison is "far-fetched". *Report of the Committee on Ministers' Powers*, Cmd. 4060/1932, p. 36.

[17] Sir William Acworth, *Elements of Railway Economics*, p. 138, quoted in Port, *Administrative Law*, pp. 136-7.

[18] See 325 *Hansard*, 3 s. 1842.

vantage of conferring greater powers on the Board of Trade."[19] The "power to remove difficulties" conferred upon the County Council by Section 80 of the Local Government Act, 1894, went through its Readings and Committee stage without serious criticism save for an indirect indictment involved in an attack upon the augmentation of bureaucratic discretion which, in the opinion of many and especially the Lords, compromised the principle of parliamentary sovereignty.[20] The debate on the Factory and Workshop Acts (Amendment) Act, 1901, illustrates strikingly Parliament's indifference or failure to understand the implications of delegated legislation. During the debate, not only was there no protest against the provisions which authorize the Home Secretary to issue Orders for the regulation of dangerous trades but members frequently insisted that the local inquiry before the issue of Orders should be dispensed with[21] and that the period of six weeks during which the draft Orders were to lie on the Table was too long.[22] The Prison Acts of 1865 and 1877 embodied numerous prison regulations in the Schedules. The Prison Act, 1898, transferred the power of making regulations for prison administration to the Home Office; these regulations were to be laid before Parliament and be subject to its disallowance within forty days. During the debate the system of Orders by the Home Department was generally hailed as a "great improvement" upon the old "inelastic" system of embodying regulations in Schedules,[23] and the particular

[19] 325 *Hansard*, 3 s. 1855.

[20] 20 *Hansard*, 4 s. 1583-4.

[21] The Home Secretary, Mr. Ritchie, emphasized the importance of the local inquiry with the "fullest publicity", but Sir Charles Dilke and Mr. H. H. Asquith regarded it as "unnecessary". 95 *Hansard*, 4 s. 112, 116, 632-3.

[22] Mr. John Burns in 95 *Hansard*, 4 s. 649.

[23] 55 *Hansard*, 4 s. 879-880, 882.

clause which effected this change of system was regarded as "the most valuable provision in the Bill." [24] The transfer of rule-making power from Parliament to the Home Department, it was said, could in no way be considered as "diminishing Parliamentary control", [25] for the Home Department was after all responsible to the House of Commons.[26] Thus, the prevailing tone of the debate, with a few insignificant exceptions,[27] was decidedly favorable to the new system of Departmental Orders.

Other Bills delegating legislative powers during this period were, however, not so well received as those we have just noted. The Poor Law Amendment Act, 1834, made a broad grant of power to the Poor Law Commissioners to make rules and regulations for the management of the poor and the administration of the laws of poor relief, with power to alter, suspend or rescind such rules. The Act "really marks the beginning of the system of entrusting delegated powers of legislation to central departments of the Government." [28] The debate on this Bill furnishes an outstanding example of the early criticism of delegated legislation. The debate in both Houses of Parliament was extremely heated. The clauses delegating powers to the Commissioners were said to be "unconstitutional" [29] and to be an abandonment of "the ancient liberties of the people." [30] "Patronage", it was said, would inevitably

[24] 55 *Hansard*, 4 s. 854.

[25] 55 *Hansard*, 4 s. 1188.

[26] 56 *Hansard*, 4 s. 77-8; 60 *Hansard* 4 s. 491; 63 *Hansard*, 4 s. 412; 63 *Hansard*, 4 s. 819.

[27] 55 *Hansard*, 4 s. 851, 847.

[28] *Committee on Ministers' Powers: Minutes of Evidence*, vol. ii, p. 3 (Memorandum of Sir Maurice Gwyer) and p. 34 (Memorandum of Sir William Graham-Harrison).

[29] 23 *Hansard*, 3 s. 959, 976, 982, 991.

[30] 23 *Hansard*, 3 s. 971.

grow out of the wide discretionary powers granted.[31] These arguments made in the House of Commons were frequently repeated by the Lords.[32] This vigorous attack, however, produced remarkable results. Lord Althorp, the Minister in charge, after making a spirited defense of the Bill, moved and helped to put through four amendments which did much to restrict the powers proposed to be granted. The effect of parliamentary criticism, therefore, was materially to hamper, if not to defeat, the purposes of the Government.

Besides the Poor Law Act, 1834, some other Bills delegating legislative powers were more or less severely attacked. Thus, the Public Health Act, 1848, which set up a General Board of Health with wide legislative powers,[33] provoked this speech:[34]

It had long being (*sic*) the pride of this country that the Government had little to do in the management of our internal affairs. The results which had happened in other countries had shown what was the inevitable tendency of placing inordinate powers in the hands of the Government. There could be no graver subject for the consideration of a legislator than what must be the necessary result of placing enormous patronage in the hands of the Executive. It was because past Parliaments had given enormous powers to the Government that he . . . had determined to use every means in his power, not merely to prevent any increase to that power, but to reduce the amount of it which the Government at present enjoyed.

[31] 23 *Hansard*, 3 s. 978.

[32] 23 *Hansard*, 3 s. 971-3.

[33] Professor Port took this Act as one of the early examples of administrative legislation and said: "... from then onwards examples tend to multiply, until we reach the present position, in which the legislation has, for a variety of reasons, been compelled to transfer to the administrative function much of what, in strict theory, it should itself perform." *Op. cit.*, p. 126.

[34] Mr. Urquhart in 98 *Hansard*, 3 s. 712.

In this protest many others joined and objections to delegated powers, though scattered, were general throughout the debate.[35] Similarly, the Railway and Canal Traffic Act, 1873, was said to be "a wholesale delegation of the powers of Parliament" which was "arbitrary" and inimical to the "liberties of the country." [36] The Electric Lighting Act, 1882, which substituted the Departmental for the Provisional Order system, was rather vigorously attacked. This change of system, it was said, was "an entirely new departure" and had the effect of permitting the Board of Trade to "usurp" the powers of Parliament.[37] Another member "regarded the adoption of the bureaucratic, or French principle of leaving everything to such a Board and its highly intelligent President, as unsatisfactory, if not unconstitutional." [38]

This brief analysis of the debates on the various Bills delegating legislative powers passed during the years between 1832 and 1906 shows that some of these Bills were very enthusiastically received by Parliament. Many were passed without adverse comment so far as their features of delegated legislation were concerned, though the general debates were lengthy and heated. There were, however, a handful of Bills the delegated legislation clauses of which formed the subject of more or less severe criticism. A majority of them were Bills that inaugurated a new principle of government or administration. The vigorous attacks upon them were therefore understandable. Moreover, these attacks occasionally persuaded the Government to yield ground to the Opposition, as in the case of the Poor Law Act, 1834.

Our second period opens with the incoming of the Liberal

[35] 98 *Hansard*, 3 s. 792, 873.

[36] 215 *Hansard*, 3 s. 351 *et seq.*

[37] 272 *Hansard*, 3 s. 567.

[38] 272 *Hansard*, 3 s. 576-577.

Government in 1906 and terminates with the outbreak of the World War. During these years the Liberal Government put through vast schemes of social and political reform which were extremely complicated and technical. Extensive and drastic powers were delegated to the Government departments and other executive authorities. The outbreak of the World War put an abrupt stop to this program of reform.

The increase in delegated legislation caused by the legislative program of the Liberal Governments after 1906 called forth a correspondingly vigorous attack. This fact appears most clearly in the debate on the Housing and Town-Planning Act, 1909, by far the most heated debate on delegated legislation before the World War. Members used most of the time at their disposal for discussion of this question, and the Second Reading was almost entirely devoted to it. It was asserted that Magna Charta and the Bill of Rights were endangered and that only Oriental despots possessed such arbitrary powers.[39] Mention was made of an " uncontrolled bureaucracy of the Local Government Board." [40] Sir Frederick Banbury, now Lord Banbury of Southam, perhaps the most vehement of the opponents of delegated legislation, asserted that " there is no doubt that the functions of the House of Commons are rapidly being taken away." [41] An interchange between a Minister and a member of the Opposition is likewise interesting: [42]

MR. JOHN BURNS: . . . in this country we are governed by Government Departments . . .

LORD ROBERT CECIL: Very nearly now.

[39] 3 H. C. Deb. 5 s. 865, 858.

[40] 10 H. C. Deb. 5 s. 31.

[41] 10 H. C. Deb. 5 s. 225-6.

[42] 10 H. C. Deb. 5 s. 250.

MR. BURNS: Subject to the House of Commons; in these administrative matters the House of Commons very wisely gives Government Departments great latitude and discretion.

The House of Commons was wise because, as Mr. Burns had said at an earlier stage of the debate: [43]

Parliament is not intended for such extra parochial matters as this. We are all Imperialists now, and Parliament ought to consider Imperial questions.

In the exceptionally prolonged debate on the National Insurance Act, 1911, furious attacks were made upon the delegation of legislative powers to the Insurance Commissioners "whom nobody knows." [44] The Government had, however, accumulated so many precedents that these arguments could almost always be met by citing some provisions in an early Act, as was done during this debate.[45] Moreover, some members believed that the complicated and technical nature of the Bill was a justification for leaving the details for the executive to take care of.[46] In spite of these arguments in support of delegated legislation, the general tone of the debate on delegated legislation was heated. Chief criticism was directed against the "undemocratic" nature of delegated legislation, which, according to the critics, shifted the responsibility of law-making from the popularly

[43] 10 H. C. Deb. 5 s. 62.

[44] 30 H. C. Deb. 5 s. 2013-4.

[45] Mr. McKenna, the Home Secretary, remarked: "I think it is perfectly safe to follow the precedents which have been laid down again and again in innumerable Acts of Parliament." 30 H. C. Deb. 5 s. 2011. After citing the Councils Act, 1888, the Local Government (Ireland) Act, 1898, and the Metropolis Water Act, 1902, Mr. Lloyd George declared: "We want to have these powers which have been in all recent Acts." 30 H. C. Deb. 5 s. 2016.

[46] 32 H. C. Deb. 5 s. 1479 and 30 H. C. Deb. 5 s. 2009, quoted *infra*, p. 113.

elected House to the uncontrolled and uncontrollable civil servants at Whitehall.[47]

Though essentially a non-contentious Bill, the Shops Act, 1912, called forth a violent denunciation from Sir Frederick Banbury, who said:[48]

> If we are to make laws, I believe it is this House that should do so . . . and we should not set up a dictator in the form of a Secretary or an Under-Secretary, and allow him to do just whatever he pleases, as long as he happens to hold office. I think that the attention of the House and of the country ought to be drawn to this because it is not the first time the Government has attempted to do it. . . . It seems to be the object of all Secretaries of State now to go beyond the province of dealing with the House of Commons and to pass Bills which will enable them to dictate the business of other people.

This summary of the debates on the clauses of delegated legislation in some of the more important Bills passed between 1906 and 1914 shows that Parliament was beginning to realize, as more and more complicated and technical legislative projects were presented, the necessity as well as the dangers and risks of the delegation of legislative powers. While the necessity of delegation was generally admitted, clauses delegating powers were often severely criticized and violently denounced. These attacks, moreover, were not monopolized by the Opposition. Members of the Government party also were alive to the dangers of excessive executive discretion and feared that the powers granted by them to their own Government might be used by the Governments of the Opposition in a way that they considered as undesirable.

The third period of our survey covers the period from

[47] 30 H. C. Deb. 5 s. 2015, 2019.

[48] 23 H. C. Deb. 5 s. 1706.

1914 down to the present time (1932). During these years England was confronted by one crisis after another, first in the trials of the World War and then in the aftermath of economic and social unrest. The emergency measures that were passed at various times delegated drastic powers to the Privy Council, the Government departments, and other executive authorities. Vast schemes of social reform, principally in the realm of local government, also delegated wide rule-making powers to the Minister of Health and local authorities.

Immediately after the outbreak of the World War, as is well-known, a series of Defense of the Realm Acts, the famous D. O. R. A., were passed by Parliament granting unprecedented powers to the Government to make rules and regulations to meet the national emergency.[49] During the passage of these Bills through Parliament, however, the consensus of parliamentary opinion was favorable. The first

[49] Much has been written about the extent and scope of these measures, which, in the opinion of some writers, swept away the "traditional safeguards" of British subjects. E. g. Lindsay Rogers, "The War and the British Constitution", *The Forum*, July, 1915. For a detailed account of the scope and operation of these measures, see J. A. Fairlie, *British War Administration*. Mr. Cecil T. Carr wrote: "Here the initial parliamentary legislation was slight, a mere pronouncement that His Majesty in Council had power to issue regulations during the war for securing the public security and the defense of the Realm.... From this grain of mustard seed sprang a goodly forest of regulations.... Who could have foreseen at the beginning that the Defense of the Realm Regulations would have embraced the acquisition of factories, the appropriation of materials ... the control of food supply and food production, the disposal of securities, the felling of timber and the taking over of mines, railways, shipping and the liquor industry? Who would have guessed that those Regulations would be extended to prohibit the holding of dog-shows, the sale of opium or the whistling for cabs in London,—all in the name of the Defense of the Realm?" *Delegated Legislation* (Cambridge, 1921), p. 18. *Cf.* Sidney W. Clarke, "The Rule of Dora", *Journal of Comparative Legislation and International Law*, 3rd series, vol. i (1919).

Act was passed without any debate whatever. When the Defense of the Realm (Amendment) Act, 1915, came up for discussion, Sir John Simon, then Attorney-General, declared: [50]

As long as the provisions of the Defense of the Realm Act as it now stands on the Statute Book give nothing more than is needed in this national emergency the argument that they are novel and do violence to our constitutional traditions is an argument of very little weight.

Sir Edward Carson deplored the talk of Magna Charta and other constitutional landmarks because he could not believe "any Government would wish to set those aside unless they thought a grave exigency has arisen." [51] The principle of ministerial responsibility, so useful in the past, was again and again exploited to justify the actions of the Government.[52] Thus, the existence of a national emergency enabled these revolutionary measures to sail through the sea of Parliament calmly and without mishap.

The Trade Boards Acts, 1918, however, caused a most heated debate on delegated legislation. Indeed, the speech for the Second Reading of the Bill by Mr. G. Roberts, the Minister of Labour, was decidedly apologetic in tone. He predicted with remarkable accuracy that the proposed substitution of the Special Order for the Provisional Order system "is likely to meet with some little criticism." [53]

[50] 70 H. C. Deb. 5 s. 289.

[51] 70 H. C. Deb. 5 s. 294.

[52] Two examples will suffice. "You must have a certain amount of confidence in your executive at a time like this." 70 H. C. Deb. 5 s. 327. "After all, the Government which exercises the power granted by the Defense of the Realm Act... is not autocratic or oligarchic Government. It is still a Government responsible to this House, and unable to carry on without the continual support of this House." 70 H. C. Deb. 5 s. 330.

[53] 107 H. C. Deb. 5 s. 63.

Most of the debate on Second Reading was concerned with delegated legislation and particularly with the relative merits of the Special and Provisional Order systems; much of the discussion centered around the question of safeguards.[54] Sir Frederick Banbury warned against "a very serious danger after the War, and that is that we shall never escape this bureaucratic octopus which is likely to cling to us after the War." [55]

In the debate on the Electricity Supply Act, 1919, a fear of the application of war-time methods to peace-time problems was frequently expressed by members of Parliament. For instance, Mr. G. Balfour said: [55]

> We are just getting out of the turmoil of the Defense of the Realm Regulations which have disgusted everybody. . . . It would be the greatest offense that could be committed against any citizen of this country to insult him by saying, "We will take advantage of the tameness and loyalty of the people during the War, and, before they recover from the shock of the War, plant 'DORA' in perpetuity upon the supply of electricity.

Likewise, in the debate on the Ministry of Transport Act, 1919, one member declared that "government by Order in Council is in war time excusable—or may be—but in peace time it is not to be endured." [56]

Many other Acts passed during these years delegated extensive powers to the Government departments, among which may be mentioned the Housing (Additional Powers) Act, 1919, the Air Navigation Act, 1920, the Seeds Act, 1920, the Gas Regulation Act, 1920, and the Roads Act, 1920.

[54] See 107 H. C. Deb. 5 s. 75, 99-100, 110, 128. For Mr. Roberts's answer to these criticisms of the proposed safeguards, see 108 H. C. Deb. 5 s. 1488 *et seq.* Some of these speeches are quoted below, *infra*, pp. 102 *et seq.*

[55] 115 H. C. Deb. 5 s. 1649.

[56] 113 H. C. Deb. 5 s. 1826.

But these Acts were essentially non-contentious. With Parliament laboring under a congested time table, the debates on them were short and the amendments to them were frequently withdrawn. In connection with the Seeds Act, 1920, however, two amendments were accepted by the Government which increased the effectiveness of the safeguards.[57]

Two Acts passed in the year 1920, the War Emergency Laws (Continuation) Act and the Emergency Powers Act, were of capital importance. It is interesting to note that Lord Hewart, then Sir Gordon Hewart, the author of *The New Despotism*, was by the irony of fate the Attorney-General of the Government and was called upon to defend the two measures before the House of Commons. The debate was not particularly furious but the view that the War had ended and that excessive executive government was alien to the Constitution was expressed by some members.[58] Sir Gordon's answer was that [59]

> these Defense of the Realm Regulations which are necessary may continue, notwithstanding that the war has practically ended. . . . With the termination of the war as a whole, the Defense of the Realm Regulations will automatically come to an end.

One of the most extensive and drastic delegations of legislative powers in recent times is the Emergency Powers Act, 1920. It has been called " the first Coercion Bill since the days of Castlereagh " which " deals the Rule of Law a death blow." " With it on the statute books Professor Dicey will have to rewrite his *Law of the Constitution*." [60]

[57] 40 H. L. Deb. 5 s. 664-666.

[58] 125 H. C. Deb. 5 s. 596, 600.

[59] 125 H. C. Deb. 5 s. 568. It is interesting to note that Lord Hewart does not comment on the war measures in his book *The New Despotism* as most other writers on delegated legislation do.

[60] W. W. Willoughby and Lindsay Rogers, *An Introduction to the Problem of Government* (New York, 1921), pp. 97 *et seq.*

The Bill was greeted with endless protests from all parts of the Houses of Parliament. The Bill, it was said, conferred "almost despotic powers" and "a dictatorship upon the Executive of the Government", at the expense of the liberty of subjects.[61] The Cabinet was said to contain "imitation Napoleons" and "Tsars"[62] who must be subjected to parliamentary control.[63] To these criticisms the Government, while emphasizing the demands of the emergency situation, retorted with the argument of ministerial responsibility. Sir Gordon Hewart pleaded that "the Executive Government must be trusted"[64] while another member declared that[65]

> Even if the Government cannot be trusted, there is a check on the Government. There is an appeal to the House of Commons, to the elected representatives of the people of this United Kingdom; and, unless they decide by their vote that such action is justified and ought to be taken, the whole of the arrangements made by the Government would fall to the ground.

As has been said, the years following the armistice witnessed a great expansion of delegated legislation. Wide and unprecedented powers to make regulations were granted to the Government departments and other authorities by a series of statutes. The Electricity Supply Act, 1922, called forth this declaration from one member of the House of Commons:[66]

> It is time that we took a decided stand to see that the views of

[61] 133 H. C. Deb. 5 s. 1592, 1805, 1808, 1826-7.

[62] 133 H. C. Deb. 5 s. 1651, 1839.

[63] 133 H. C. Deb. 5 s. 1419, 1826-7.

[64] 133 H. C. Deb. 5 s. 1664.

[65] 133 H. C. Deb. 5 s. 1647.

[66] 154 H. C. Deb. 5 s. 185.

the people shall prevail and be pressed in this House, to compel both the Executive and the Government to obey this House, and not for this House to be absolutely controlled by the Executive.

The London Traffic Act, 1924, was the occasion for a long discussion of delegated legislation in both Houses of Parliament, during which an amendment was carried against the MacDonald Government. But in the House of Lords, the Bill was restored to its original form. The powers proposed to be delegated to the Minister of Transport were characterized as "very autocratic" and the Minister was said to be "a sort of traffic Mussolini, or superman, with tremendous powers."[67] The proposed Traffic Advisory Committee of nineteen, according to some members, represented "bureaucracy *in excelsis*"[68] and it was the duty of Parliament to protest against any form of "Whitehall Government."[69] Similar arguments were used in the House of Lords when a heated debate also took place on the Bill.[70] The Government resorted to old arguments in refutation of these charges: for instance, Mr. Sidney Webb, President of the Board of Trade, applied the theory of ministerial responsibility in a rather novel way when he said:[71]

The one thing which we ought to preserve is that the House should have authority over the Minister responsible, and you cannot have that unless the responsible Minister has himself authority within his own sphere.

[67] 171 H. C. Deb. 5 s. 1713. The extent of the powers proposed to be granted by this Bill may be gathered from the statement of Mr. Percy Harris who found that the Minister was mentioned no less than 69 times in the Bill. 175 H. C. Deb. 5 s. 280.

[68] 175 H. C. Deb. 5 s. 1751. *Cf.* 175 H. C. Deb. 5 s. 1774.

[69] 171 H. C. Deb. 5 s. 1738.

[70] 58 H. L. Deb. 5 s. 811, 879-880, 882.

[71] 175 H. C. Deb. 5 s. 281.

Lord Newton remarked humorously that "if we cannot get rid of the Minister of Transport, surely the best we can do is to make use of him." [72]

The prolonged debate on the Rating and Valuation Act, 1925, contained the old arguments against delegated legislation. The Bill, for instance, was assailed as being "undemocratic", "bureaucratic", and "repugnant to every section of the best feeling in this country." [73] The Board of Guardians (Default) Act, 1926, was debated at great length. An amendment requiring an affirmative resolution by the House of Commons to make regulations valid was supported by no less than twelve speeches, only to be defeated in the Division Lobbies after Mr. Neville Chamberlain, the Minister of Health, declined to accept it.[74] The Road Transport Lighting Act, 1927, was greeted, according to one member, with "an almost universal criticism of the powers being given to the Minister *carte blanche*." [75] This statement was more than borne out by the numerous and persistent protests registered in the *Debates*.[76]

It remained for the Local Government Act, 1929, to give us the most hotly contested debate on delegated legislation on record. This fact is by no means an accident. The Bill involved not only the fundamentals of governmental policy but was both instructive and unusual in the extent to which it delegated legislative powers to the Ministry of Health.[77]

[72] 58 H. L. Deb. 5 s. 458.

[73] 188 H. C. Deb. 5 s. 1913, 2745.

[74] 197 H. C. Deb. 2442 *et seq*. *Cf*. also same volume 1691-2, 1747-8 (Mr. Ramsay MacDonald), 2391, 2429.

[75] 204 H. C. Deb. 5 s. 1616.

[76] 204 H. C. Deb. 5 s. 1587, 1595, 1614.

[77] Thus one member testified: "I have taken the trouble to analyse this Bill, and I find that from cover to cover there are 134 references either to Orders which have been made by the Minister, or to schemes prepared for his sanction, or to directions that he must make, or to

It is indeed most difficult, if not impossible, to give a summary of this remarkable debate. Suffice it to say that every provision delegating rule-making powers to the Ministry of Health or to local authorities was hotly debated and bitterly contested. The "power to remove difficulties" clause (Section 130) was especially resented by the members. Amendment after amendment was put on the paper and pressed to the Division Lobbies; speech after speech was made in support and in denunciation of these amendments. The attack was led chiefly by a group of lawyers, with Sir Henry Slesser, later Lord Justice Slesser, at their head. They styled themselves the "watchdogs of the Constitution" and

regulations that he may draw up." 223 H. C. Deb. 5 s. 147. Put in a more humorous way, another member said: "I want to draw attention to the variations on the theme of bureaucratic control which are in this Bill. References are made once to the following powers of the Minister: I begin to think that there is one shrine in the Ministry of Health, and that is 'power', and one hymn of praise, the theme of which is, 'The Minister, always the Minister'. The Minister 'may declare', 'may decide', 'may consult', 'may alter', 'may extend', 'may consent', 'may confirm', 'may correct', 'may formulate', 'may dispense with', 'may cause investigation into', 'may increase to 50 per cent the fees for births, marriages or deaths'—so that he will be dealing with us after we have gone, if unhappily we pass before the first quinquennium is over—he 'shall give an opportunity', and he 'may make an equitable adjustment'. Twice references are made to 'may have representations made' and to 'shall pay'. He may 'reduce the grants' twice. He may 'make a report to the Ministry of Transport' three times. He may 'have a grievance sent to him' three times. He may 'have copies of agreements sent to him' four times. He may 'sanction' four times. He 'shall publish in one or more local newspapers' four times. He may 'consider' five times. (Laughter) . . . He 'may be satisfied' five times. He may 'appoint an arbitrator' five times. He may 'be applied to' or 'appealed to' three times. He may 'allow" seven times. He may 'hold an inquiry' seven times. He may 'direct' eight times. He may 'certify' ten times. He may 'make regulations' ten times. He may 'approve or issue new powers' 14 times. He may 'determine" 20 times. There are 91 references in the Bill to the making of Orders by the Minister. That makes 231 variations on one theme." 225 H. C. Deb. 5 s. 852.

appealed to all members of the House, regardless of party affiliations, to stand together in a desperate fight against ministerial and bureaucratic encroachments.[78] The defense was largely taken up by Mr. Neville Chamberlain, the Minister of Health, and Sir Kinsley Wood, his Parliamentary Secretary, both of whom cited numerous precedents to justify their demands for legislative powers.[79] The stubbornness of the Government in refusing to yield ground to the Opposition even in the minutest details was indeed surprising, and, thanks to party regularity, no amendment of any importance succeeded in getting through. This debate on the Local Government Bill, 1929, marks the climax of opposition to delegated legislation in the history of English lawmaking.

The Factory and Workshop (Cotton Cloth Factories) Act, 1929, originated in the House of Lords. In that House Lord Banbury made an attack upon the whole system of delegated legislation: [80]

> This Bill perpetuates a vicious principle which unfortunately has grown very much in the last few years. It gives power to a Department to usurp the functions of Parliament, and to pass what they call regulations which have the effect of an Act of Parliament, and deal with His Majesty's subjects; in fact, this does what in days gone by caused a King to lose his head.

Lord Carson joined in this general attack and said that the Minister "is put in a position over both Houses of Parliament and over the King." [81] Based as it was upon a Report of a Departmental Committee, the Bill was not debated in the House of Commons.

[78] 225 H. C. Deb. 5 s. 610-611.

[79] 224 H. C. Deb. 5 s. 976 *et seq.*

[80] 72 H. L. Deb. 5 s. 932-3.

[81] 72 H. L. Deb. 5 s. 936.

The difficulties caused by the economic depression in England from the middle of 1930 gave rise to the " National Government " under Mr. Ramsay MacDonald. The Government's demand for " a doctor's mandate " was granted by the English people when an overwhelming majority of the " National " members were returned in the November Elections. In carrying out the " doctor's mandate ", the Government introduced and put on the statute books a series of six emergency measures, all of them delegating wide rule-making powers on matters of principle or of taxation.[82] The Opposition being small and more or less unorganized, these measures passed through their various stages without much difficulty. The majority of the members held that these exceptional measures were occasioned and justified by the emergency. Even Mr. Arthur Henderson considered that delegation of legislative powers was necessary provided " they are given under proper conditions, and if they are properly used." [83] Prime Minister MacDonald justified the procedure of Orders in Council because the emergency made the maintenance of normal procedure not only undesirable but also impossible.[84] But criticisms of this invasion of Parliament's prerogative were not lacking. Many members saw in these measures the forerunner of a dictatorship fashioned upon the models of those " National Governments " on the Continent, which were using " Facist methods " to " ignore the methods of democracy and of Parliamentary

[82] The series of five Acts are: The Gold Standard (Amendment) Act, 1931; The National Economy Act, 1931; The Foodstuffs (Prevention of Exploitation) Act, 1931; The Abnormal Importations (Customs Duties) Act, 1931; The Horticultural Products (Emergency Customs Duties) Act, 1931, and The Import Duties Act, 1932. A brief summary of the powers delegated by these Acts is found in *Report of the Committee on Ministers' Powers,* Cmd. 4060/1932, pp. 33-6.

[83] 256 H. C. Deb. 5 s. 1303.

[84] 256 H. C. Deb. 5 s. 419.

procedure." [85] The power given to the Government to impose duties on importations by the Abnormal Importations (Customs Duties) Act and the Horticultural Products (Emergency Customs Duties) Act were characterized as "revolutionary" and "unconstitutional" and as inimical to the principles of democracy and of the Bill of Rights.[86] The Labour Opposition also made the threat that if the National Government effected its legislative program by Orders in Council the Labour Party might not forget to make use of the same device "to nationalise the mines and innumerable other public undertakings." [87] The Import Duties Act, 1932, which the Committee on Ministers' Powers considers as "obviously one of the most important delegating enactments which Parliament has ever passed",[88] was debated at length in Parliament. Though the issue of protection and free trade was the major issue between the Treasury and the Opposition Benches, the delegation of wide rule-making powers to the Treasury, the Board of Trade and the Import Duties Advisory Committee was regarded by some members as "whittling away the rights of Parliament" [89] and as handing over the powers of this House to an arbitrary and autocratic body." [90]

With the exception of D. O. R. A. and a few consolidation Bills, all these delegating measures, emergency and reform alike, went through a very trying parliamentary ordeal. The powers proposed to be delegated were conceded most reluctantly by Parliament and the clauses which

[85] 256 H. C. Deb. 5 s. 466-7.

[86] 259 H. C. Deb. 5 s. 728-9.

[87] 256 H. C. Deb. 5 s. 436, 467.

[88] *Report of the Committee on Ministers' Powers*, Cmd. 4060/1932, p. 36.

[89] Mr. Price in 262 H. C. Deb. 5 s. 287.

[90] Mr. Mason in 262 H. C. Deb. 5 s. 294.

effected the delegation were usually ruthlessly denounced. The climax of parliamentary criticism of delegated legislation was reached, as has been said, during the debate on the Local Government Act, 1929, especially when the "power to remove difficulties" clause was under discussion. The outburst of Parliamentary oratory against delegated legislation was evidence that Parliament had become extremely jealous of its own powers and was trying to make a last and desperate stand against the menacing growth of delegated legislation. The length as well as the vigor of the debates compares favorably with those of the years immediately preceding the World War and presents a totally different picture from the debates in the years 1832 and 1906.

This brief historical survey of parliamentary opinion of delegated legislation from its beginnings one hundred years ago shows that the comparative indifference of the years 1832-1906 was transformed into increased vigilance during the period preceding the World War and culminated in a great outburst of criticism and attack during the years that followed the armistice. In the first period, delegated legislation had not become "an active habit." The dangers and risks which it involved were still unknown to the average members of Parliament. Moreover, during this "golden age of parliamentary government", Parliament was still confident of its own "omnipotence and omnicompetence." Unlimited confidence was, therefore, placed in the Ministers chosen from among its own members. The Civil Service, in fact and in theory, was still subject to the caprice of its political chiefs, but confidence in the Ministers meant confidence in the Civil Servants. Phrases like "the dictatorship of the Cabinet" or the "bureaucracy of Whitehall" were still unheard of. The investment of important rule-making powers in the hands of the Ministers and the Civil Servants was thus made without serious question.

The second period presents a different picture. The powers of the executive government increased so rapidly that Parliament began to lose faith in itself. It began to shy at the menace of ministerial and bureaucratic encroachments. As more and more legislative powers slipped from its hands, Parliament sought to tighten its grip. Criticisms of delegated legislation were profuse and amendments providing for better safeguards and for more control became abundant.

Our third period witnesses the increasing jealousy of Parliament of executive usurpation of its own powers. With the exception of the Defense of the Realm Acts, even emergency measures could not get through without being attacked. The other measures suffered the constant denunciation of the Opposition, and, in some cases, of members of the Government party itself. Amendment after amendment and speech after speech were made in an attempt to mitigate, if not to refuse, the powers which the Government proposed to be delegated.

But this awakening came too late. Debate in the House of Commons had been seriously curtailed by the adoption of the closure. The House of Lords had ceased to be an important cog in the legislative machine. Above all, party fealty had become so stringent that the slightest deviation from the course marked out by the party leaders savored of betrayal and revolt. In the halcyon days of parliamentary government criticisms had been sufficiently effective to cause the Governments to retreat, as in the case of the Poor Law Act, 1834; the much more vehement attack upon the Local Government Bill, 1929, was able to eliminate only one word from the Government draft, and an unimportant word at that. After twelve vituperative speeches against a single clause in the Board of Guardians Act, 1926, the majority filed into the Government Lobby as if nothing had happened. To be sure the MacDonald Government were defeated upon a clause delegating legislative powers in the London Traffic Act, 1924, but they were a minority Government, and did not resign on account of the defeat. Indeed, since 1906, it has been rare for a member of Parliament, charmed by heroics and eloquence, to vote against his own party upon the issue of delegated legislation.

CHAPTER III

Parliamentary Criticisms of Delegated Legislation

We doubt . . . whether Parliament itself has fully realised how extensive the practice of delegation has become, or the extent to which it has surrendered its own functions in the process, or how easily the practice might be abused.

Report of the Committee on Ministers' Powers, Cmd. 4060/1932, p. 24.

Now is it, or is it not, tolerably certain that the majority in Parliament were not aware of any such provision in the Bill when they passed it, and that very few of those who were aware of it had any knowledge of its effect?

Lord Hewart, *The New Despotism*, p. 73.

It may be doubted whether the average member of Parliament has any conception of the length to which a device, within limits commendable, has surreptitiously been carried.

J. A. R. Marriott, "Whitehall and Westminster', *Edinburgh Review*, January, 1926.

The preceding chapter presented a historical sketch of the criticisms and justifications by members of Parliament of clauses in Bills delegating in one way or another to the Privy Council, the Government Departments or other executive agencies powers to make rules and regulations having the force of law. As a historical sketch, it has proceeded in a chronological fashion beginning from about 1832 and extending down to the present day. It is the purpose of this and the following chapters to analyze the arguments of members against clauses delegating such powers, and to show the methods by which Parliament attempted to minimize, if not to check, the dangers of abuse inherent in the practice.

The general subject of delegation of legislative powers had

called forth many severe criticisms from members of Parliament. The extensive powers delegated by the Poor Law Act, 1834, to the Poor Law Commissioners were said to be "kingly, judicial, legislative, and administrative . . . beyond precedent and public safety "[1] and to be such as even " the King or Parliament separately did not possess ".[2] Mr. Balfour characterized the powers proposed to be granted by the Destructive Insect and Pest Act, 1907, as "unknown powers " and ventured " to . . . protest against this method of legislation ".[3] Sir Frederick Banbury's remarks in connection with the Housing and Town-Planning Act, 1909, the Shops Act, 1912, and the Factory and Workshop Act, 1929, have been elsewhere noted.[4] They form the most severe indictment of delegated legislation and were matched only by the more succinct denunciations of Sir Henry Slesser, now Lord Justice Slesser, parts of whose innumerable speeches will be presently cited.

On March 27, 1929, in the debate on Adjournment for Easter Recess, Sir John Marriott made a long speech attacking the whole practice of delegation of legislative and judicial powers. His remarks on delegated legislation deserve to be quoted extensively. He said:[5]

[1] 23 *Hansard,* 3 s. 955.

[2] 23 *Hansard,* 3 s. 954.

[3] 174 *Hansard,* 4 s. 562.

[4] See *supra,* pp. 51, 53, 62. *Cf.* 72 H. L. Deb. 5 s. 1187.

[5] 226 H. C. Deb. 5 s. 2507 *et seq.* This debate was the result of a question addressed by Sir John to Prime Minister Stanley Baldwin on February 25, 1929. In his long speech Sir John quoted from many authors, Sir Courtenay Ilbert and President Lowell, and cited some *obiter dicta* in recent cases. Marriott's voluminous works on English political history and governmental institutions all register his profound indignation at delegated legislation. See, for instance, his *The Mechanism of the Modern State* (Oxford, 1927), vol. ii, pp. 236-7, and his introduction to the third edition of his *English Political Institutions* (p. xli) in which he said: "The multiplication of statutes almost inevitably tends

> . . . the position in which we find ourselves amounts to nothing less than an abdication on the part of Parliament of its supreme legislative function . . . it was the traditional method of English legislation to provide by Statute, as far as possible, beforehand for every contingency which could be expected to arise. As a result of this, the form of English Statutes was exceptionally detailed and elaborate . . . during the last 20 years . . . we have moved and are moving more and more rapidly . . . towards Continental methods. Many of our modern Statutes are mere skeletons of legislation. They afford really no adequate idea of their ultimate scope. They lay down a few general rules, and then they leave it to the appropriate Government Department to give substance to the legislative skeleton by the issue of administrative Orders. This growing tendency has been noted by all the more responsible commentators on English law and English constitutional procedure. . . . The danger we have to face at present is . . . the wholesale delegation to the administrative Departments of legislative, or quasi-legislative powers, which ought to be exercised only in Parliament itself or, to put it at the lowest, under the closer scrutiny and supervision of Parliament. That is the curse of delegated legislation. . . . That is the legislative danger, the danger of a rapidly accumulating mass of statutory Rules and Orders of which Parliament has really only a formal cognisance. . . .

In the debate on the Local Government Act, 1929, Sir John likewise made a vigorous attack the tone of which was not unlike the one just quoted.[6]

to the curtailment of individual liberty, but liberty has been curtailed even more perhaps by the character than by the volume of legislation.... Bacon observed that there is 'no worse torture than the torture of laws.' If he was right the modern citizen is evidently obnoxious to that form of torture to a degree undreamed of by the victims of medieval tyranny." Professor C. K. Allen commented on the opinion of Sir John in *Bureaucracy Triumphant* (London, 1931), pp. 26-7.

[6] "I look upon (delegated legislation) as an exceedingly mischievous tendency in modern legislation. I think this House has been far too careless in regard to the way in which it has given powers of subordinate

One of the chief criticisms of delegated legislation is that it violates some of the basic principles of the English Constitution and is detrimental to the hard-won liberties of English subjects. The powers proposed to be delegated by the Poor Law Act, 1834, were said to be "most unconstitutional" and "hitherto unknown to the British Constitution".[7] "Delegating the authority of the Legislature in that way", one member asserted, "was foreign to the Constitution of the country".[8] Lord Wynford declared in the House of Lords:[9]

Never was there an instance in either ancient or modern times when such a power as this was given to any set of men. Blackstone himself contemplated with horror the power that was given to the King under the Mutiny Act. He thought it was *unconstitutional* that His Majesty should have the power of making laws, deciding upon laws, and rescinding laws; and yet the power which Blackstone thought unfit to be placed in the hands even of the King was to be given to these Commissioners. . . .

Sir Frederick Banbury, in the debate on the Housing Act, 1907, thought that placing powers in the hands of a Minister "is subversive of all Parliamentary Government, and is a greater alteration in the Constitution than if the Finance Bill

legislation to departments of the State. Not once but over and over again in recent legislation this House has parted with powers which indisputably belong to Parliament alone. Legislation is one thing and administration is another. In this House we are concerned with legislation, and I think, speaking generally, that any tendency is deplorable which gives over to the administrative side of public departments functions which ought to be jealously retained in the hands of this and the other House of Parliament." 225 H. C. Deb. 5 s. 594.

[7] 23 *Hansard,* 3 s. 976.

[8] 23 *Hansard,* 3 s. 991.

[9] 25 *Hansard,* 3 s. 260-1. Italics mine.

is rejected in another place." [10] "The almost despotic power" placed upon the Government by the Emergency Powers Act, 1920, was described as at variance with the basic principles of the English Constitution.[11] The powers conferred upon the Ministry of Health by the Board of Guardians (Default) Act, 1926, were said to have outraged "the commonly accepted application of the Constitution of this Country." [12] A note of party warfare was struck when another member attacked the Conservative party then in power by saying that "there is an extraordinary habit among Conservative Ministers, who are supporters of the Constitution, to brush aside all constitutional practices and constitutional theories when they find they cannot get something exactly as they wish it." [13] Mr. W. Bennett, in the course of the debate on the Local Government Act, 1929, made an appeal to all members of Parliament, regardless of party affiliation, to regard themselves as "the guardians of the Constitution" in order to resist the spread of delegated legislation.[14]

[10] 10 H. C. Deb. 5 s. 1674-5. Sir Frederick, in the debate on the Trade Boards Act, 1918, asked: "Why not pass a single Bill, saying, 'Ministers can do no wrong'?" 108 H. C. Deb. 5 s. 1495.

[11] 133 H. C. Deb. 5 s. 1592.

[12] 197 H. C. Deb. 5 s. 2421.

[13] 197 H. C. Deb. 5 s. 2424. A similar instance of party criticism was made during the debate on the Abnormal Importations (Customs Duties) Act, 1931, when one member, after describing the Bill as "altogether wrong", "revolutionary", "unconstitutional and unparliamentary", said: "In the country the Conservative party go around boasting that they stand for the Constitution, and are always trying to create the impression that the Labour party want to overturn the Constitution, yet now we find the Conservatives using the most unconstitutional methods in connection with these Orders in Council." 259 H. C. Deb. 5 s. 1084.

[14] Mr. Bennett said: "In the last few years, there has been a growing tendency to give greater and greater power to Ministers and administrators, and . . . the power of Parliament is being trespassed upon more and more. I do not like taunts addressed to us about constitu-

Englishmen are prone to boast of the "ancient liberties" which their forefathers won and which are chronicled in the glorious pages of their history. These "liberties" were said to have been violated by the vicious practice of delegated legislation. Magna Charta and the Bill of Rights might be overridden if the Ministers, armed with enormous powers granted by Act of Parliament, were disposed to disregard them.[15] The Emergency Powers Act, 1920, was asserted to have enabled the Ministers to rescind the guarantee contained in these documents.[16] It became the duty of Parliament to protect them from being molested.[17]

The fruits of the bloody struggles in the time of the Stuart Kings, embodied in the Bill of Rights, had done away once and for all with the suspending and dispensing powers of the King. The Local Government Act, 1929, was said to have revived these powers, this time not in the hands of a Stuart King but in those of a Minister, who for the time being, occupied the position of the Minister of Health.[18] Although

tionalism. I believe that we on this side are the guardians of the Constitution, and I have been given to understand that, regardless of party, all Members put the power of Parliament as their first consideration, and stand for its preservation even if they have to vote against their own party. . . . We are witnessing the growing power of Ministers and Departments to go behind the back of Parliament and make orders which constitute legislation in essence. It is time that some sort of stand was made against it." 225 H. C. Deb. 5 s. 610-11.

[15] 3 H. C. Deb. 5 s. 858.

[16] 133 H. C. Deb. 5 s. 1592.

[17] 133 H. C. Deb. 5 s. 1826-7.

[18] 224 H. C. Deb. 5 s. 970-1. *Cf.* also 73 H. L. Deb. 5 s. 610. Sir John Marriott, in his book *The Crisis of English Liberty: A History of the Stuart Monarchy and the Puritan Revolution* (New York, 1930), expresses the opinion that the problems of the seventeenth century have re-emerged today because of the growing practice of delegated legislation. Professor Robert L. Schuyler, in a review of this book in the *Political Science Quarterly* for June, 1931, summarizes his opinion by saying that Marriott "points out that the constitutional problems of the seventeenth

the whole fabric of English Government had undergone a momentous change since the days of the Stuarts and the Minister of the day is now responsible to the House of Commons—a characteristic which distinguishes him essentially from an irresponsible monarch—Mr Gerald Hurst found that a historical analogy could still be drawn at the expense of the Minister of Health. He declared: [19]

I think we have good grounds also for distrusting any repetition in these days of the dispensing and suspending power. . . . The ground on which the dispensing power was justified by the judges of that day [before 1688] was that the divine right of kings entitled the King to fill up such gaps as had been left by Parliament, and that it was a necessary and proper exercise of such divine right. We do not want to substitute for the divine right of kings the divine right of the Minister of Health.

Sir Alfred Hopkinson found that the Local Government Act, 1929, had wrought " an unconscious revolution ".[20]

It is obviously declaring that we are to give the Minister a dispensing power over Acts of Parliament. We thought we had got rid of all that in the time of James II, and I do not want to see in any Act of Parliament a declaration that the constitutional principles which were established in 1688 are overridden.

One of the most cherished rights of Parliament was its power of taxation. When the Poor Law Act, 1834, was

century, long supposed to have been permanently solved, have re-emerged of late as living issues, that 'under conditions greatly altered and in forms not always recognizable, devices adopted by the Stuart Kings in their contest with Parliament and in their relations with the Judges are today making an unwelcome reappearance' . . . Sir John resorts to the seventeenth century to find precedents for liberty in much the same spirit that seventeenth century libertarians invoked the Lancastrian Constitution against *their* 'new despotism'."

[19] 225 H. C. Deb. 5 s. 609.

[20] 224 H. C. Deb. 5 s. 986-7.

under discussion, one member asserted that "delegating the power to impose taxes on the subject to certain Commissioners to be appointed by Parliament" was "a power unknown to the Constitution".[21] In the debate on the Imports and Exports Regulation Bill, 1919, Lord Robert Cecil made the point of order that "it is a fundamental rule that this House does not delegate its power of taxation."[22] Mr. Attlee, in the debate on the Emergency Tariff Bill, 1931, declared that[23]

> the right of determining taxation is one of the most vital rights of the House. Years ago the issue was fought out, as between Parliament and the Executive, as to who should have the right to tax the subject, and Parliament won. The Executive at that time was the Crown. The Executive at this time is the Cabinet, but the principle is precisely the same. That great fight was fought over the Bill of Rights.

Speaker Lowther, ruling upon the point made by Lord Robert Cecil, said:[24]

[21] 23 *Hansard*, 3 s. 959.

[22] 122 H. C. Deb. 5 s. 212.

[23] 259 H. C. Deb. 5 s. 729.

[24] 122 H. C. Deb. 5 s. 213. Professor Harold J. Laski inveighed against the procedure of Order in Council adopted by the National Government in the crisis of 1931 and after. "On the ground of emergency", he wrote, "the new government has taken power to effect the economies it deems necessary, not by the normal channels of debate in the House of Commons (with the use, if need be, of closure and guillotine), but by Order in Council. They have thereby overthrown, at a stroke, the result of the historic struggle in this country to place the control of expenditure in the hands, not of the Executive, but of Parliament. I cannot easily conceive a more dangerous precedent for the future. Broadly, Mr. MacDonald invites any government which deems itself confronted by an emergency, and does not desire to be hampered by discussion, to take such powers for action as will destroy all discussion save that represented by the possibility of a prayer against an Order in Council moved after 11 o'clock. It is grave, indeed, that the House of Commons should be deprived of its power over expenditure; but it is urgent to remember that what has been applied to

It has been part of the unwritten law of Parliament that the goods upon which and the rates at which taxes are to be levied shall be fixed and determined by the House of Commons itself. I am not prepared to say that the House cannot delegate that power to some other body. . . . I will only say that at present I am not aware of any similar case.

The theory of separation of powers was sometimes used as an argument against delegated legislation.[25] It was invoked in 1834 by a member in an attack upon the Poor Law Act of that year. He said:[26]

Why, what was the Constitution? . . . Was not one of its principles, that the legislative, the administrative, and executive powers of the country should be separate? Had they not at all times, when free government was recognized, felt a great jealousy in intrusting these powers into the same hands? . . . Until this Bill, no one ever heard of such a combination of legislative, administrative, and executive powers, in any State pretending to freedom. What was the definition of a tyrant? Was it not

expenditure to-day may easily be applied to taxation to-morrow." "British Crisis of 1931", *Political Quarterly*, Oct.-Dec., 1931. As Professor Laski points out the power conferred by the Emergency Tariff Bill of 1931 was not strictly the power of taxation although he suggests the implications of this new method to that power. Mr. Runciman, President of the Board of Trade, also made this point. "What is handed over to the Board of Trade is not a power to impose taxes. It is a power to initiate the procedure by which taxes will be imposed. It is a power of initiation which the Government is asking the House to place in the hands of the Board of Trade and, when the Board of Trade had taken the initiatory steps, the sanction of Parliament must be obtained within 28 days." 259 H. C. Deb. 5 s. 724.

[25] The bearing of the theory of separation of powers upon delegated legislation is generally recognized by writers on the subject. *Cf.* William A. Robson, *Justice and Administrative Law* (London, 1928), introduction; F. J. Port, *Administrative Law* (London, 1929), ch. iii; and *Report of the Committee on Ministers' Powers*, Cmd. 4060/1932, pp. 8 *et seq.*

[26] 23 *Hansard*, 3 s. 982.

that of one who could make laws and execute them, or unmake and change them, at his own will and by his word? The Commissioners were to have this power. . . . Why, he saw no difference between the power of any arbitrary despot, and that of the Commissioners.

In the debate on the Board of Guardians Act, 1926, one member applied the theory of checks and balances in an attempt to defeat the Bill.

It is the habit of the British Constitution [he asserted] to introduce checks and balances. We do not believe in unrestricted power. The Constitution as it stands at present does not believe in unrestricted power. This House, sovereign though it ought to be, is restricted to some extent by certain restraints and vetoes. If there is a case for restraint upon the power of the sovereign House of Parliament, there ought to be some restraint upon the power of the Minister. . . .[27]

Among the sacred principles of the British Constitution the doctrine of parliamentary sovereignty occupies a high place. The critics of delegated legislation took it as one of the chief arguments against delegating legislative powers to the executive. In the *Parliamentary Debates* one finds frequent

[27] 197 H. C. Deb. 5 s. 2427. The theory of parliamentary sovereignty has a long history in English political thought. Sir Thomas Smith, in his *De Republica Anglorum* written in 1583, declared that Parliament "representeth and hath the power of the whole realme both the head and the bodie." Alston Ed., p. 49. A saying commonly attributed to de Lolme is that Parliament has the power to do anything but make a man a woman. The theory was most clearly defined by Professor A. V. Dicey in his classic treatise *The Law of the Constitution* (London, 1915). In the light of these assertions the passage just quoted seems contradictory. An even queerer statement was made during the debate on the Prison Act, 1898, when one member said that the Bill, far from taking powers from Parliament, "will give Parliament the power, *which it does not now possess,* of considering and co-operating with the Home Office in the consideration of prison treatment." 55 *Hansard,* 4 s. 1187. The italics are mine.

assertions that Parliament, being " sovereign " in the British body politic, should not part with powers which it has so long enjoyed.[28] Sir Henry Slesser who is in that group of lawyers who described themselves as " the watchdogs of the Constitution ", defined their position in these words:[29]

Parliament, and Parliament alone shall define beyond any doubt of any sort the limits within which the present law shall be altered.

It is the privilege of Parliament to legislate, not the privilege of the Executive, and people here and outside are constantly calling attention to the fact that this Legislature is giving to the Executive power after power which ought to be kept in the hands of Parliament itself. If Parliament is prepared to part with this privilege. . . . I say that all legislation in the future really becomes quite vain.[30]

Perhaps the most interesting argument directed against delegated legislation was that used by some members who contrasted the relatively simple procedure by which an Act could be changed at the " sweet will " of a Minister or a Government department and the long and dilatory process by which a Bill might be amended in the House or in Committee.[31]

[28] See, for instance, 324 *Hansard,* 3 s. 1117 *et seq.* and also 327 *Hansard,* 3 s. 636-7 for opinions expressed in connection with the Local Government Act, 1888.

[29] 225 H. C. Deb. 5 s. 590.

[30] 224 H. C. Deb. 5 s. 974-5.

[31] In connection with the Local Government Act, 1929, Colonel Wedgwood said: "We have spent 12 days on the Bill in Committee alone discussing it [Clause 111], hardly amending it, but still altering it in some details, and yet for the next two years the Ministry of Health can amend what Parliament has passed. . . . Parliament ought not to abrogate its powers in this way." 224 H. C. Deb. 5 s. 980-1. Mr. Rye, in the same debate said: "The real issue is whether we are to continue to sacrifice rights which we possess. Are we going to spend our time day after day debating Bills and discussing Clauses in Committee, and, after assisting to put Bills on the Statute Book, ought we to leave a

Many members considered that delegated legislation, by transferring the power to make laws from the popularly elected Parliament to the executive, violated the principle of democracy which was one of the basic principles of the English Constitution. Many clauses delegating powers to the executive were described by members as " undemocratic " and therefore " unconstitutional." [32] In close relationship to this was the fear of the decline of the authority of Parliament in favor of " a dictatorship of the Cabinet ", or even of one

loophole for a Minister at his own free will to alter those Acts of Parliament in such a manner as he may think fit? Under those circumstances, we might as well shut up the House of Commons. We attend this House in order to debate, discuss, and frame Measures before they become Acts of Parliament, and, if we insert a Clause enabling Ministers to alter those Acts, we might as well stay away altogether." 224 H. C. Deb. 5 s. 989.

[32] The following is a list of some of the examples of this line of attack as employed by members of Parliament. In connection with the National Insurance Act, 1911, Mr. C. Bathurst called the clause delegating authority a "most unfortunate and undemocratic precedent". 30 H. C. Deb. 5 s. 2019. Sir Frederick Banbury described the procedure of Special Orders proposed by the Government in the Trade Boards Act, 1918, as not being a democratic principle. 108 H. C. Deb. 5 s. 1492. Mr. Pringle said that it was destroying "every shadow of democratic control over Ministerial acts by our present legislation". 108 H. C. Deb. 5 s. 1499. The method of Orders in Council proposed in the Ministry of Transport Act, 1919, was characterized as "undemocratic" while the imposition of adequate safeguards on these Orders to be issued under the Electricity Supply Act, 1919, would "go back to the sound principles of democratic control". 117 H. C. Deb. 5 s. 861 and 115 H. C. Deb. 5 s. 1677, 1259. The Rating and Valuation Act, 1925, was denounced as "entirely undemocratic" and "repugnant to every section of the best feeling in this country". 188 H. C. Deb. 5 s. 2745. The Board of Guardians (Default) Act, 1926, was said to "strike at the very root of what we believe to be democratic government, namely powers to suppress a popularly-elected representative body"—the Board of Guardians. 197 H. C. Deb. 5 s. 2319. Mr. Neville Chamberlain, the Minister of Health who introduced the Local Government Act, 1929, was described by Mr. T. Williams as "one of those few people who still think that democracy is a failure in this or any other country." 224 H. C. Deb. 5 s. 835.

man.[33] The fears that were expressed at Westminster were of these three varieties. In the *Hansard* are found numerous instances in which the Minister was said to possess powers comparable to those of the " despots " and " autocrats " of ancient times and " dictators " of the present age. He was compared to Julius Caesar,[34] the Roman Dictator,[35] Judge Jeffreys,[36] Kings Louis XIV, XV and XVI of France,[37] Napoleon,[38] the Czar,[39] Mussolini,[40] Primo de Rivera,[41] the

[33] Among the treatises on the British Constitution in recent years much had been said on this subject. The decline of Parliament and the dictatorship of the Cabinet were emphasized as representing one of the most important changes in the twentieth century. Prominent students of English political institutions, among them Sir Sidney Low, President Lowell and Sir William Anson, had written about the decline of Parliament. "The British Cabinet . . . has come to lead rather than to follow the House; to rule it rather than to obey it." Willoughby and Rogers, *An Introduction into the Problem of Government* (New York, 1921), p. 308. *Cf.* Robert L. Schuyler, " The Decline of the House of Commons ", *Columbia University Quarterly*, October, 1919; H. J. Laski, "The Mother of Parliaments ", *Foreign Affairs*, July, 1931; James K. Pollock, Jr., "The Position of the British Parliament ", *American Political Science Review*, August, 1931.

[34] 10 H. C. Deb. 5 s. 28.

[35] 23 *Hansard*, 3 s. 971.

[36] 10 H. C. Deb. 5 s. 1675.

[37] Sir Frederick Banbury made most of these interesting comparisons. After charging Mr. John Burns with being a Judge Jeffreys, a characterization which Mr. Burns instantly refused to accept, he compared him to Louis XVI, changed to Louis XV later on, only to find in the end that Louis XIV was the most appropriate man for the occasion. 10 H. C. Deb. 5 s. 79, 1675.

[38] 133 H. C. Deb. 5 s. 1651; 224 H. C. Deb. 5 s. 824.

[39] 133 H. C. Deb. 5 s. 1839.

[40] The Mussolini analogy was immensely popular in the House of Commons and his name was frequently mentioned, e.g., 197 H. C. Deb. 5 s. 1777; 171 H. C. Deb. 5 s. 1713; 197 H. C. Deb. 5 s. 2391; 224 H. C. Deb. 5 s. 824.

[41] 225 H. C. Deb. 5 s. 278.

Shah of Persia,[42] and the Sultan of Turkey.[43] The powers conferred on the Commissioners by the Poor Law Act, 1834, were described as "tyrannical" and "despotic".[44] The Board of Guardians Act, 1926, aroused the fear of a "system of dictatorship which is now applying in one or two countries across the channel", and of the installation of a Mussolini in the Ministry of Health.[45] "It is the inherent vice [of dictatorship]", Sir John Marriott said, "that though you may provide for the perpetuation of autocracy you cannot guarantee the continuance of benevolence."[46] Finally, Sir Henry Slesser attacked the whole system of delegated legislation as "a kind of despotic tyranny under the form of law."[47]

On the problem of bureaucracy and government by experts, it may be said that British mentality is in general hostile to encroachments by permanent officials whose acts are not subject to popular control.[48] The practice of delegated leg-

[42] 3 H. C. Deb. 5 s. 858.

[43] 10 H. C. Deb. 5 s, 190.

[44] 23 *Hansard,* 3 s. 984.

[45] 197 H. C. Deb. 5 s. 2429.

[46] 225 H. C. Deb. 5 s. 882.

[47] 225 H. C. Deb. 5 s. 588.

[48] The evils of bureaucracy were discussed in general terms, with special reference to British conditions, by Ramsay Muir in his *Peers and Bureaucrats* (London, 1910), pp. 1-94. He discussed the subject further, though more concisely, in his recent book *How Britain is Governed* (New York, 1930), ch. ii. Sir Courtenay Ilbert found that "Englishmen have a deep-seated distrust of official discretion, a deep-seated skepticism about bureaucratic wisdom." *Legislative Methods and Forms* (London, 1901), p. 39. Sir Courtenay drew a distinction between "government by experts" and "government with the aid of experts". He resented vigorously the former but admitted the necessity of the latter. *The Mechanics of Law-Making* (New York, 1914), p. 76. Henry Sidgwick dissented from Walter Bagehot's defense of amateur government in a declaration that "it is difficult to believe that any business can be under the best attainable management when the chief

islation, unfortunately, meant the investment of tremendous powers in the hands of the heads of Government departments, who, as was generally admitted, relied to a considerable extent upon the permanent officials in the formulation of their general policies.[49] Thus these permanent officials were those

who has the whole responsibility of action lacks the knowledge and experience requisite for wise and independent decisions." *The Elements of Politics* (London, 1891), p. 423. "Englishmen had developed," Herman Finer discovered, "an exceptional sensitiveness to bureaucratic pretensions . . . a strong feeling against bureaucracy existed, and coloured thought about the Civil Service." *Theory and Practice of Modern Government* (London, 1932), vol. ii, p. 1171. Professor Laski inveighed against expert government in an article and predicted that "government by experts would . . . mean after a time government in the interests of the experts. Of that the outcome would be either stagnation, on the one hand, or social antagonism, upon the other." "The Limitations of the Expert", *Harpers Magazine*, December, 1930. C. K. Allen also feared the increased powers of the Civil servant. *Bureaucracy Triumphant* (London, 1931), pp. 1 *et seq.* Sir Maurice Gwyer, in his memorandum submitted to the Committee on Ministers' Powers, dwelt at length on this subject and defended the permanent officials against these charges. He thought that charges of any abuse of delegated powers should be made against the Minister who was responsible to Parliament rather than against the Civil servant who was responsible only to the Minister. "The popular portrait of the Civil Servant," Sir Maurice continued, "avid of power and unscrupulous in his manner of attaining it, is to those who know the facts so remote from real life as to be almost laughable." Citing the number of letters that certain important Government departments received everyday, he attempted to prove that "Civil Servants have not the time, even if they had the desire, to devote their energies to the acquisition of power for the purpose of harassing the King's subjects." Finally, "the alleged antagonism between the administrator and the law in my experience simply does not exist. The administrator has the same respect for the law as the average Englishman, and neither consciously nor unconsciously seeks to set himself aside it or above it." *Committee on Ministers' Powers: Minutes of Evidence*, vol. ii, pp. 1-2.

[49] This fact was dwelt on effectively by Colonel Wedgwood during the discussion of the Local Government Act, 1929, when he said: "In this Bill we talk of the Minister, we see him before us, and we think of him as the devil of the piece; but we know that he really is not. We know that he is merely the brocaded porter at the entrance to the

who finally exercised these "dangerous" powers, a fact to which the average Englishman, that is to say the M. P., with his traditional antipathy toward bureaucratic government, never failed to object. The attack on delegated legislation, therefore, was focused in the opposition to the permanent official or bureaucrat. He was often pictured as a man so concerned with technicalities and details that he often failed to see the woods for the individual trees. He was also looked upon as being eager to snatch governmental powers from the Ministers and to wield them at the expense of the liberty of British subjects. Time and again, in the discussion of delegated legislation, attacks on the increased powers of the Ministers, and thus of the bureaucrats, were repeated, reiterated, emphasized, amplified.[50]

However, this line of attack came late. As the preceding chapters has shown, there was very little, if any, fear of bureaucratic encroachments in the days when delegated legislation was still in its infancy. On the contrary, powers were entrusted to the Government departments without question because the members of Parliament had full confidence in the permanent officials themselves.[51] It was not until the end

cinema, that the picture palace is behind, and that there are the people who, concealed behind the term 'the Minister', are being given powers to override Parliament. This is an age when the bureaucracy are constantly grasping more and more power, becoming more and more dictatorial. We not only get autocrats and dictators in the South of Europe, but we invest our permanent officials with all the powers of a dictator, though without the title." 224 H. C. Deb. 5 s. 982.

[50] Sir Frederick Banbury, for instance, declared that "the fewer officials we have the better" while another member confessed that he had "no faith whatever in the Departments". 130 H. C. Deb. 5 s. 361 and 135 H. C. Deb. 5 s. 2646-7. There were attacks on "bureaucracy of Whitehall", of "bureaucracy *in excelsis*", of "a bureaucrat's paradise", etc. 197 H. C. Deb. 5 s. 2435; 171 H. C. Deb. 5 s, 1751; 223 H. C. Deb. 5 s. 271.

[51] For example, as late as 1882, in the debate on the Electricity Lighting

of the last century that the fear of bureaucracy became apparent, a beginning destined to attain greater heights in the days to come. In connection with the Local Government Act, 1894, Lord Salisbury and Mr. A. J. Balfour each made a lengthy speech in a succinct attack on bureaucracy. The bureaucrats, according to these critics, "absolutely depend upon the beck and call of the Departmental Chiefs"[52] who were party politicians[53] so that "great cases of corruption and partiality will come in."[54] Both speakers warned against further extensions of the Powers of the bureaucrats because such extensions would become "the germ from which a great evil will grow",[55] and because the bureaucrats "might be drawn from that perfectly straight and impartial course which they would otherwise take."[56] The defense against these attacks was taken up principally by Mr. H. H. Fowler, the President of the Local Government Board, and Sir William Harcourt, the Chancellor of the Exchequer, who declared that it was contrary to the traditions of English politics to question the integrity of the Civil Service of the Crown —an argument which was immediately challenged by Mr. Balfour.[57] Apart from the fact that party capital might have

Act, one member testified that "minor officials" in the Board of Trade were loath to extend their powers without limit". 272 *Hansard,* 3 s. 589-90. See, however, 272 *Hansard,* 3 s. 576-7.

[52] 20 *Hansard,* 4 s. 1584.

[53] 20 *Hansard,* 4 s. 1584.

[54] 20 *Hansard,* 4 s. 1584.

[55] 20 *Hansard,* 4 s. 1583.

[56] 21 *Hansard,* 4 s. 612.

[57] Sir William Harcourt said: "If it is to be said that the permanent Civil Service of the country are incompetent because they are appointed by a politician, you will cast a reproach over the whole Civil Service which is undeserved; and . . . it is destructive of the whole organization of your Government." 21 *Hansard,* 4 s. 618. Mr. Fowler "resented very strongly the . . . suspicion that the Local Government Board would be influenced by political reasons in these matters." 20 *Hansard,*

been made from this question of bureaucratic encroachments, the sentiments which were expressed by Lord Salisbury and Mr. Balfour were shared by a substantial portion of British opinion.

In the period after the World War, bureaucracy formed the subject of almost continuous attack on Bills containing provisions for delegated legislation. The bureaucrats were said to regard "the House of Commons as nothing but a nuisance." [58] In the eyes of a Laborite, Miss Lawrence, a bureaucrat was fundamentally conservative in outlook and would oppose any innovation proposed by the progressives.[59]

She inveighed against [60]

4 s. 1098. Mr. Balfour retorted that "the doctrine . . . that it is contrary to the traditions of English politics to attack Civil servants of the Crown, is not a doctrine which has been almost consistently maintained by those who now support it." 21 *Hansard*, 4 s, 612.

[58] 175 H. C. Deb. 5 s. 386. Professor Laski, in his article just cited, contrasted the qualities of a statesman with those of an expert and concluded "*Expertise* . . . sacrifices the insight of common sense to intensity of experience. It breeds an inability to accept new views from the very depth of its preoccupation with his own conclusions. It too often fails to see round its subject. It sees its results out of perspecive by making them the center of relevance to which all other results must be related. Too often, also, it lacks humility; and this breeds in its possessors a failure in proportion which make them fail to see the obvious which is before their very noses. It has, also, a certain caste-spirit about it, so that experts tend to neglect all evidence which does not come from those who belong to their own ranks. Above all, perhaps, and this most urgently when human problems are concerned, the expert fails to see that every judgment he makes not purely factual in nature brings with it a scheme of values which has no special validity about it. He tends to confuse the importance of his facts with the importance of what he proposes to do about them." *Harpers Magazine*, December, 1930. *Cf.* Miss Ellen Wilkinson's note to the *Report of the Committee on Ministers' Powers*, Cmd. 4060/1932, p. 138.

[59] She said: "As a matter of historic fact, nearly every improvement which we have now in local life, has been originally the creation of some locality with expansive ideas, and has nearly always been disliked by the Government Department." 224 H. C. Deb. 5 s. 830.

[60] 224 H. C. Deb. 5 s. 831.

the extraordinary expansion of bureaucracy and . . . the extension of the power of the Minister, sitting *in camera*, at Whitehall. Those are bad things. . . . The expansion of bureaucracy is a very great evil.

Another member announced that he would [61]

continue to oppose such an extension of bureaucratic control [as proposed by the Local Government Act, 1929]. While I have every respect for the expert I object to be governed by the expert when I have no control over the expert.

An interesting aspect of this general attack upon bureaucracy was the mutual accusations by the Socialists and the Conservatives that the others were in favor of bureaucratic control. Thus, Mr. Arthur Greenwood, the Labor member, maintained " that the real friends and creators of bureaucracy in this country are the Tory Party ",[62] a charge to which a Conservative member retorted [63]

[61] 224 H. C. Deb. 5 s. 836.

[62] 223 H. C. Deb. 5 s. 2854. Professor Finer found that there was a general hatred on the part of the Tories of bureaucracy. He said: "Most people who are well endowed with all that they want in terms of wealth, education, and pleasure, are inclined to insist that they are better let alone. It cannot be denied that Toryism is embraced and propagated by such people. They are not ungenerous in unprompted giving, that is, when they may do as they like to do; but State command is anathema. Hence the Tory hatred of officialdom, which it calls and teaches others to call, Bureaucracy: less competent than private people, usurpers, eaten up with routine, dangerous to liberties, extravagant! " *The Theory and Practice of Modern Government,* vol. i, p. 522.

Mr. Lansbury, in a speech, attacked Mr. Neville Chamberlain who was then the Minister of Health in charge of the Local Government Act, 1929, saying that during the whole administration of Mr. Chamberlain the policy had been to arm the Minister with more powers so that he " could cripple and hinder Socialists and Labour men who might desire to extend social services in directions to which the present Minister of Health objects, and he would be able to prevent them from carrying out their policy." 224 H. C. Deb. 5 s. 816-8.

[63] 225 H. C. Deb. 5 s. 608.

It seems to me, also, that in their denunciations of bureaucracy, hon. Members opposite [the Socialists] forget what would happen if a system of State Socialism were ever established. It would simply involve the enthronement of the bureaucracy which they now denounce.

In the debate on "parliamentary control" which took place on April 4, 1917, strong resentment was shown against the growth of bureaucracy. One member said: [64]

the power of the permanent officials of the Civil Service is becoming too prominent a feature . . . it would be a source of disaster if Civil servants were allowed to extend the control which they already possess. A great deal has been said recently about the danger of autocracies, but I believe that an autocratic dynasty is even more desirable than a bureaucratic executive.

Another member added: [65]

We have certainly not gone to war with Prussia in order to capture its Constitution. It would indeed be the irony of fate if we liberated Germany and enslaved ourselves, and if at the same time that we were Anglicising Prussia we found that we had Prussianised England.

In their attacks on delegated legislation, the arguments which we have just analyzed and presented were sometimes severally used and sometimes combined by members of Parliament. Thus bureaucratic control was often regarded as being in its very nature undemocratic.[66] Again, it was

[64] 92 H. C. Deb. 5 s. 1364.

[65] 92 H. C. Deb. 5 s. 1385.

[66] Colonel Wedgwood said: "Nearly all the changes proposed are for greater bureaucratic control. . . . You are getting away from the direct representation of the people and getting instead, more and more, the co-opted expert, who would not be answerable to public opinion." 223 H. C. Deb. 5 s. 272. Mr. Ernest Brown predicted that the "next fight this nation and this House will have to undertake will be a fight to control the bureaucracy, both in its growth in size and its growth in

asserted that the abrogation of parliamentary sovereignty meant the establishment of an autocratic government.[67] The whole practice of delegated legislation was said to lead to bureaucratic control. The vesting of powers in the executive was regarded as a revival of the suspending and dispensing powers which once cost a King his head. By delegated legislation, in short, the whole fabric of the British constitution was put in jeopardy, and nothing short of a complete abolition of this practice would satisfy those who called themselves the " watchdogs " or " guardians " of the constitution, whether they were Socialists or Conservatives. Delegated legislation was " a great evil " and, as such, must be resisted and halted. The members who were alarmed by the enormous growth of delegated legislation could muster writers from Blackstone to Lord Hewart to support their thesis. The lawyers, especially, could cite not only the names of illustrious constitutonal lawyers but also those of the learned members of the Bench whose *obiter dicta* very often confirmed their opinion. John Morley once said that " the opinion of Parliament is the opinion of yesterday, and the opinion of judges is the opinion of day before yesterday." Lawyers, trained and versed in the writings of their predecessors are as a rule more conservative than men outside of the legal profession.[68] It was the lawyers in Parliament

power, which menaced democratic government in this country." 224 H. C. Deb. 5 s. 814. The granting of powers to the departments was said to be granting powers "over the democracy, over this unfortunate people." 224 H. C. Deb. 5 s. 982.

[67] Major Price said: "I agree that it is necessary to lessen the burdens that are placed upon Parliament, but there is something that is even more necessary, and that is the elimination of the risk of autocratic power on the part of any Minister to alter the provisions of an Act of Parliament." 225 H. C. Deb. 5 s. 613.

[68] "Lawyers are by training, and usually by temperament, conservative in their outlook. Some generations have now been nurtured on the doctrines of Parliamentary Sovereignty and the Rule of Law." E. C. S.

who resented delegated legislation most. The temptation is hard to resist to interpret Morley's epigram in terms of Burke's jibe that " the generality of people are fifty years, at least, behind hand in their politicks."

Wade and Godfrey Phillips, *Constitutional Law* (London, 1931), p. 101. Indeed, it can be said that most of the critics of delegated legislation, both in Parliament and in academic circles, belong to the legal profession or are students of law. Among students of English government who have dealt with this problem, however, the attitude is generally more dispassionate and detached, although Sir John Marriott here forms an exception.

CHAPTER IV

The Demand for Safeguards

Nothing is so dangerous in a democracy as a safeguard which appears to be adequate but is really a façade.

Miss Ellen Wilkinson, *Report of the Committee on Ministers' Powers*, Cmd. 4060/1932, p. 138.

In so far as delegated legislation contains the germ of arbitrary administration, every possible safeguard must be devised.

Cecil T. Carr, *Delegated Legislation*, p. 26.

The preceding chapter has shown that some members of Parliament see in delegated legislation a vicious practice so open to abuse that nothing short of its extirpation will remedy the evil. Whether inclined to agree with this view or not, all Governments, whatever their composition, have availed themselves of the powers thus granted and have asked for more. Together with a large group of members the Governments hold the view that the tide can no longer be turned. They are rather inclined to see in the delegation of legislative powers a useful, nay an indispensible, instrument of government. They are, however, also attached to the traditional principles of parliamentary sovereignty and the rule of law. Consequently they wish to preserve to Parliament its ancient powers and privileges and to maintain the judicial power of independent scrutiny. The problem, then, becomes one of maintaining the practice of delegated legislation while hedging it about with such safeguards that the executive will be discouraged from abusing its powers and that such abuses as result can be easily and effectively redressed.

Between the die-hards and the majority group the difference is that while the former will be content with nothing less than the restoration of Parliament's " legislative monopoly ", the latter seek only the creation and maintenance of a real and effective control by Parliament and the courts over the executive. Despite this difference in ideals the two groups are frequently allied on the principle that half a loaf is better than no bread. Hence the persistent demand for more adequate safeguards.

The increase in the powers of the executive with its attendant dilution of the traditional authority of the House of Commons has aroused considerable discussion both within and outside Parliament. For instance, in 1917, there was a debate in Parliament on the general subject of "parliamentary control" in the course of which strong manifestations of resentment against the dictatorial methods of Mr. Lloyd George's War Cabinet appeared.[1] In the seventeenth century phrase of Dunning, Sir Herbert Samuel declared that "the influence of the House of Commons had diminished, was diminishing, and ought to be increased."[2] Sir C. Henry contended that "the position of the rank and file of Members of Parliament of both Houses is an anamalous one. . . . Members of Parliament are no longer able to exercise the functions which the electorate rely upon them to do."[3] This lamentable situation called for a remedy which Sir C. Henry professed to find in the French system of parliamentary commissions.[4] But this suggestion was not accepted. Able arguments were made against it.

[1] See 92 H. C. Deb. 5 s. 1363 *et seq.* for this interesting debate.

[2] 92 H. C. Deb. 5 s. 1369. *Cf.* J. A. R. Marriott, "Law and Liberty", *Fortnightly Review*, July, 1928.

[3] 92 H. C. Deb. 5 s. 1363.

[4] See an interesting discussion of this proposal in Lindsay Rogers, "Parliamentary Commissions in France", *Political Science Quarterly*, December, 1923, where the pros and cons of such a translation of the French system to England are discussed at length. There is also a short discussion in Ramsay Muir, *How Britain is Governed* (New York, 1930), pp. 230 *et seq.*

The demand for parliamentary control did not end with this rejection of the French system. In the debates on Bills containing delegating clauses, demands for more adequate parliamentary control were frequent. Parliament, it was said, "ought to retain as much control over legislation as is practically possible."[5] "I would like," said another member, "to see the maximum Parliamentary control retained."[6]

The reasons urged by members in support of their persistent efforts to retain or regain control over delegated legislation were many and varied. One of the principal arguments made was that the safeguards commonly provided were inadequate and insufficient to prevent abuses by the executive of the powers granted. In the opinion of one member, there were two circumstances likely to defeat the purpose for which Orders were required to be placed on the Table for a definite period:[7]

> In the first place, such a scheme might lie on the Table and arrest no attention; . . . secondly, the scheme might arrest attention, but that hon. Members might be unable to get any opportunity of discussing it. This difficulty was much larger under the new Rules than under the old, and . . . there was no guarantee . . . that the Government of the day might not on their own motion put schemes on the Table . . . without Parliament having an opportunity of discussing them.

The safeguard was, therefore, "a complete illusion",[8] a "Ministerial camouflage"[9] and "no Parliamentary check whatever".[10] "To say that Parliament has a power of

[5] 224 H. C. Deb. 5 s. 984 (Local Government Act, 1929).

[6] 225 H. C. Deb. 5 s. 629.

[7] 327 *Hansard*, 3 s. 636-7.

[8] 10 H. C. Deb. 5 s. 203 (Housing and Town Planning Act, 1909).

[9] 107 H. C. Deb. 5 s. 128 (Trade Boards Act, 1918).

[10] 225 H. C. Deb. 5 s. 278 (Local Government Act, 1929).

veto," Mr. H. H. Asquith asserted, "is to pay lip homage to Parliament and not to give it any really effective control." [11] This was true because, as Sir Frederick Banbury contended,[12]

> Hardly anyone knows that the Order has been made. The debate cannot come on until after eleven o'clock. It is almost impossible to get a quorum, and when you do, especially in these days [during the War], as the number of Members present after eleven o'clock is rarely over 120, I do not think it is very often that the Government has enough Members to put the Closure on. It is perfectly evident that with eighty-eight Gentlemen who are committed to a policy, and can only oppose it by resignation, this safeguard [of 40 days] is absolutely illusory.

Therefore, as one member naively remarked, these Orders might just as well be laid in the library or in the Ministry concerned.[13] Another member even suspected that the Minister might lay the Orders on the Table just before the Summer Recess and thus deprive Parliament of the chance to present an Address against them, although this was decidedly not the customary practice.[14] In sum, parliamentary congestion, together with the Rules of the House of Commons which were but the outcome of such congestion, had made the laying of Orders on the Table of the House an ineffective safeguard.[15]

[11] 133 H. C. Deb. 5 s. 1419 (Emergency Powers Act, 1920).

[12] 107 H. C. Deb. 5 s. 110 (Trade Boards Act, 1918). In 1898, when the Prison Act was being discussed, one member said: "In practice... the only opportunity [to present an address] is after twelve o'clock at night. But it would be monstrous to ask the House of Commons to discuss such Rules as these after twelve o'clock." 56 *Hansard*, 4 s. 111.

[13] 225 H. C. Deb. 5 s. 278 (Local Government Act, 1929).

[14] 107 H. C. Deb. 5 s. 75 (Trade Boards Act, 1918).

[15] *Cf.* an interesting remark in 225 H. C. Deb. 5 s. 626.

The Rules in the House of Lords, however, present a different picture. There the private members are not so oppressed and the Closure is never applied. Contrasting the conditions in the two Houses, Lord Banbury said: [16]

It took me about twenty years to find out where these notices were, then I found them in the desk of the Clerk at the Table. In order to get at them you had to ask him to open his desk, which was probably full of other things. Then perhaps the Speaker would address him, and he had to ask you to wait. It was very difficult to get them, and after you had them you could only move in the matter after eleven o'clock at night, when nearly everyone has gone, and if attention was called to the fact that there were not forty Members present, the whole thing was over. In this House [Lords] it is quite different. You can find out where the notices are, and move them at a reasonable time. So far as this House is concerned there is some protection, but none in the House of Commons.

Theoretically, as Prime Minister Baldwin said, " it is open to any Member of Parliament, while such Rules or Orders lie on the Table of the House, to move for their annulment on the ground that they are inexpedient or unjust, or upon any other ground he pleases." [17] As a matter of fact, however, this possibility remained theoretical. " Within the last thirty-five or forty years," one member observed,[18]

I have seen literally thousands of Orders in Council laid upon that Table. I never saw a Debate on an Order in Council unless it referred either to theology or to Ireland. These subjects

[16] 72 H. L. Deb. 5 s. 1191-2. Lord Banbury quoted Lord Hugh Cecil who said: " Nobody knows anything about it, it can only come on after 11 o'clock, and no one knows where to find it."

[17] Mr. Baldwin in an answer to a question addressed to him by Sir John Marriott, February 25, 1929. 226 H. C. Deb. 5 s. 24.

[18] 113 H. C. Deb. 5 s. 1787 (Ministry of Transport Act, 1919).

always attract a crowded House. On all other occasions when an Order in Council has been put upon the Table I have seen the unfortunate and despairing Member trying to keep a House and usually failing, and the Government Whips taking very good care he did not get a quorum. If he did the Government Whips put the credit and existence of the Government against his objections.

Party ties were perhaps the greatest obstacle to the effective working of these safeguards. A private member, urged on by " outside organisations affected by these Rules and Orders ",[19] might be interested in annulling one or two of these Orders but any attempt to do so against the will of the Government to the support of which he was pledged meant revolt or betrayal, entailing consequences the gravity of which was sometimes too heavy to be borne. Thus one member declared: [20]

I am not making any party point about mechanical majorities . . . but any party when faced by a *fait accompli,* by something which had been put into operation by the Minister, would be extremely reluctant to vote an Address which would be in effect a vote of censure on what he had done.

Even in the House of Lords where, as Lord Banbury said, it was much easier to present an Address than in the House of Commons, it was very seldom done. Earl Beauchamp asserted pathetically that: [21]

[19] Mr. Baldwin in an answer to a question addressed to him by Sir John Marriott, February 25, 1929. 226 H. C. Deb. 5 s. 24.

[20] 224 H. C. Deb. 5 s. 985. The Orders to be issued by the Ministry of Health under authority of the Local Government Act, 1929, would go into effect the moment they are issued and in case a resolution praying for annulment were carried in the Houses, these Orders will be annulled but such annulment is not retroactive. The same is true with the Orders to be issued under the Board of Guardians Act, 1926.

[21] 54 H. L. Deb. 5 s. 309 (Salmon and Freshwater Fisheries Act, 1923).

When once . . . these public Departments are persuaded, whether rightly or wrongly, that the Order is one which ought to be made, no amount of protest in this House is likely to persuade your Lordships to withold your assent.

" Ministers come and Ministers go." In the change of Ministers is to be found another reason for more adequate safeguards.[22] Ministerial differences in temperament, viewpoint, diligence and efficiency result in different uses of the powers granted and so may let in abuses. Safeguards against the effects of such varieties are needed.

" It must be remembered," one member reminded the Commons.[23]

that there is not only the possibility that different Ministers with different ideas will administer these provisions, but also that there are different principles on which they may be administered.

It is interesting to note that this fear for a change of Ministry

[22] This fact had been repeatedly pointed out in the Houses of Parliament. In 1834, during the debate on the Poor Law Act, one member said that "he had the greatest respect for His Majesty's present Ministers, but changes would take place." 23 *Hansard*, 3 s. 974. In 1901, in connection with the Factory and Workshops Acts Amendment Act, one member declared that the powers "might safely be left in the hands of the present Home Secretary; but in future Home Secretaries the House may not have the same confidence." 95 *Hansard*, 4 s. 129. "The Secretary to the Board of Education" at the time of the Education Act, 1902, "might be very reasonable, but someday the position might be very different." 114 *Hansard*, 4 s. 799. After describing the powers proposed to be given to the Minister of Transport by the London Traffic Act, 1924, as "autocratic", Mr. Percy Harris said that "after all, Ministers come and go". 171 H. C. Deb. 5 s. 1713. Mr. Attlee said that "Ministers come and Ministers go, and he may be succeeded by someone of an extreme red tint, or an extreme white tint." 197 H. C. Deb. 5 s. 2425 (Board of Guardians Act, 1926). Similar ideas were expressed in the same debate by Mr. Thurtle. 197 H. C. Deb. 5 s. 2426. The Local Government Act, 1929, called forth the same argument from Mr. Arthur Greenwood. 224 H. C. Deb. 5 s. 810.

[23] 224 H. C. Deb. 5 s. 824.

was not confined to the Opposition Benches. When an amendment was proposed abolishing the two forms of safeguards provided by the Local Government Act, 1929, Sir Kingsley Wood, Parliamentary Secretary to the Ministry of Health, said:[24]

There are different kinds of Ministers of Health. I can conceive of a very different Minister of Health from the present one [Mr. Neville Chamberlain], and he might have a very different idea as to how he should put this Clause into operation. . . . From that point of view, these considerable powers should not be left in the hands of the Minister of Health without any guidance at all.

Another argument which has been used against the practice of laying Orders on the Table is that these Orders, once they have been drafted by the departments, are not subject to amendment by Parliament; Parliament had either to accept or to reject them as a whole. Thus, during the debate on the Prison Act, 1898, one member said:[25]

We have had placed before us a Bill which empowers the Home Secretary to draft the Rules, and we are called upon to accept or reject that empowering enactment without having any opportunity afforded us of dealing with the Rules which are the subject-matter of this Measure, or criticising them to the fullest extent as we might if we had the Rules themselves embodied in the Bill . . . We have no means of considering, changing, or modifying *seriatim* the Rules. . . . I say that Parliament is derogating from its functions in allowing permanent officials to formulate Rules, and leaving itself only the power of petitioning against the Rules.

This argument would appear to be a most devastating criti-

[24] 224 H. C. Deb. 5 s. 803-4.

[25] 55 *Hansard*, 4 s. 847. Later on in the debate, another member said that "the House may object to what appears in the rules, but it will have no opportunity . . . of introducing anything." 56 *Hansard*, 4 s. 111.

cism of this particular form of parliamentary safeguard if the facts are as presented. But it is the practice of Parliament to allow the Orders on the Table to be amended in the same way as they can be annulled,[26] a fact which takes away entirely the wind from the sails of this argument.

The charge was also made that the record of Ministers and their departments in exercising the powers delegated to them had been a bad one. Such an accusation was made by Sir William Harcourt against the Board of Education in connection with the Education Act, 1902.[27] Since it had misused the powers delegated to it previously, its demand for more powers should not be granted. Ministers, moreover, when asking Parliament for powers, had given assurances which, once the powers were granted, they ignored in the exercise of the authority delegated. The Trade Boards Act, 1918, was the subject of the following comment: [28]

> Our experience of the past few months proves most conclusively that the action of the Government bears no kind of resemblance to the professions under which it gets powers it asks for.

The provision for maternity and child welfare in the Local Government Act, 1929, elicited a similar declaration from Miss Ellen Wilkinson. Mr. Neville Chamberlain, the Minister of Health, had issued some " milk circulars " of which Miss Wilkinson disapproved. She, therefore, objected to the grant of further powers to Mr. Chamberlain on the ground that there was no assurance that he would exercise them wisely.[29]

The debates upon delegated legislation, then, centered

[26] E. g. a Rule issued under the Nurses' Registration Act, 1919, was amended by the House of Commons in 1923. *Journal of the House of Commons*, vol. 178, p. 210.

[27] 113 *Hansard*, 4 s. 392.

[28] 108 H. C. Deb. 5 s. 1484.

[29] 224 H. C. Deb. 5 s. 510-1.

around the necessity for parliamentary control and the effectiveness of the means employed to assure it. The efficacy of existing safeguards was said to be imperiled by the Rules of the House and the actual working of that body; criticism was made of the lack of guarantees that powers would be exercised in accordance with the purpose for which they were granted;[30] and, finally, the relation between parliamentary confidence in the Government and the activities of the departments was shown to be, to say the least, so remote that the whole assumption that parliamentary control was assured by the principle of ministerial responsibility collapsed.

The suggestions as to the form the increased safeguards should take have been many. The device most commonly urged has been the system of Provisional Orders. Provisional Orders must be confirmed by Act of Parliament before they take effect—the necessity for confirmation, it is said, leaves to Parliament an effective measure of control over the executive which drafts these Orders. Against the adoption of this system there was raised the objection that it was cumbersome, often costly, and always slow. Statutory Rules and Orders, on the other hand, could be issued in a very short time and took effect when issued. The relative merits of the two forms of Orders were repeatedly debated in the Houses of Parliament. The opponents of all delegation, as might be expected, prefer the Provisional Order.

The original draft of the Local Government Act, 1888, provided in Clause 8 for the transfer by means of Orders

[30] Mr. Ramsay MacDonald said: "This Bill [the Board of Guardians Act, 1926] gives him [the Minister of Health] a power which he can use in a thousand and one different ways.... Is he aware of the fact that under the general words which he uses to take this power, he can use this power in the way exactly opposite to the way in which he proposes to use it here? That is exceedingly bad legislation. It is a very bad model of a Bill or an Act when one party brings it in to suit its purpose and another party can administer it for exactly the opposite purpose." 197 H. C. Deb. 5 s. 1747-8.

in Council of certain powers then possessed by the Treasury, the Local Government Board and the Board of Trade to the newly created County Councils as and when these Councils should be organized and ready to assume these powers. No question of delegation was involved in this provision for the powers proposed to be transferred had already been delegated to the Government departments. There was, however, in the course of the debate a general discussion of the methods by which the powers could be transferred which deserves careful analysis. First, these powers, already delegated to the departments, might be transferred to the County Councils by Acts of Parliament which would embody the detailed procedure and date of transfer in the Schedules of the Act. Those who believed that Parliament ought to lay down general principles on a matter of such "political importance" and that there was no other way in which Parliament could effectively supervise the transfer of powers advocated this method.[31] Second, these powers might be transferred by Orders in Council, as provided in the draft; these Orders would be laid before the House for forty days. According to the spokesman of the Government, Mr. Ritchie, this method had the twofold advantage of sparing the Committee of the Whole House "a long and very technical and intricate discussion"[32] and of effecting the transfer as soon as such transfer was considered desirable.[33] Third, the transfer could be effected by means of Provisional Orders, "involving the necessity of a confirming Bill." The advocates of this method urged that the necessity of confirmation guaranteed that the matter would arrest the attention of Parliament.[34] The Provisional Order system was found by Mr.

[31] 324 *Hansard*, 3 s. 1135-6.

[32] 327 *Hansard*, 3 s. 631.

[33] 327 *Hansard*, 3 s. 1014-5

[34] 327 *Hansard*, 3 s. 636.

Hobhouse to be surrounded " with safeguards in all particulars ",[35] and Sir William Harcourt regarded it as being " nothing more or less than . . . another Act of Parliament under another name." [36] Mr. Chaplin offered statistical evidence to prove that the method had worked satisfactorily in the past.[37] The arguments in support of the Provisional Order system were so cogent that Mr. Ritchie was won over and brought to maintain that it was the method best suited to the complicated problems of local government.[38] Some members, however, remained unconvinced and characterized the proposals to effect the transfer by other means than Acts of Parliament as " very mischievous." [39]

The debate on the Trade Boards Act, 1909, found the Government in the unusual position of a champion of parlia-

[35] 327 *Hansard*, 3 s. 649.

[36] 327 *Hansard*, 3 s. 1001.

[37] He said: " He would like to call attention to the fact that, out of 256 Provisional Orders moved by the Board of Trade with regard to tramways, 242 had been actually carried; out of 279 Provisional Orders in the matter of Gas and Water, 276 had been carried—that was to say, out of a total of 535 Provisional Orders, 518 had been carried. That was very strong testimony to the admirable way in which these matters had been dealt with by the Department up to the present time." 327 *Hansard*, 3 s. 998. President Lowell found that " practically . . . they [the Provisional Orders] are almost always confirmed without amendment." Lowell, *Government of England* (New York, 1908), vol. i, p. 365. *Cf.* figures in Marriott, *The Mechanism of the Modern State* (Oxford, 1927), vol. i, p. 522 and vol. ii, p. 377.

[38] Mr. Ritchie said in part: " There were many adjustments which would be necessary, and which he thought could only be adequately treated by means of investigation. This investigation would, of course, be secured by means of a Provisional Order. The proper course, therefore, to pursue would be to deal with this matter by means of a Provisional Order." 328 *Hansard*, 3 s. 1280.

[39] Thus one member said: " Practically no one was aware of what was being done when measures of this kind were passed. Provisional Order Bills were placed on the Table at the time of Private Business; nothing was said about them and hardly anybody knew what they were." 327 *Hansard*, 3 s. 653.

mentary control against the encroachments of the departments. The Opposition moved to amend the Bill by substituting the Departmental for the Provisional Order system. The Opposition assailed the Provisional Order as "unnecessarily cumbersome and costly" and favored the Departmental Order as not only "much swifter" but also backed by "Parliamentary power by reason of the fact that the Order must lie on the Table of the House for 40 days." [40] The Parliamentary Secretary of the Board of Trade, Mr. H. J. Tennant, defended the Provisional Order system in the following terms: [41]

It is perfectly true . . . that this procedure of coming to Parliament for a Provisional Order may be more costly and more expensive and may occupy more time, but it need not occupy more time and it need not be more cumbersome or expensive. . . . The Provisional Orders which have been made by the Board of Trade in the 10 years from 1899 are as follows: there have been Orders applied for to the extent of 1,160. Orders made by the Board of Trade 1,032, Orders confirmed by Parliament 1,011, Orders opposed in Parliament 97; so that the Provisional Order procedure need not be, and is not in the majority of cases, half so cumbersome or expensive as [it was thought to be].

The Government, of course, prevailed.

The Provisional Order system defended by the Government in 1909 was abandoned by it in 1918. The Trade Boards Act of that year substituted the Special Order for the 1909 procedure. The Opposition now advocated the Provisional Order.[42] The question provoked a hot debate which it seems worthwhile to analyse.

[40] 7 H. C. Deb. 5 s. 2430-1.

[41] 7 H. C. Deb. 5 s. 2433.

[42] Clause 2, sub-section (1) reads: "Every special order shall without confirmation by Parliament have effect as if enacted in this Act..."

The Special Orders which the Bill proposed to introduce were to be issued by the Board of Trade subject to the usual safeguard of forty days on the Table of the House. The Government argued that the new system would "save time" [43] and that the safeguard of forty days would ensure parliamentary control.[44] These arguments were, however, met point by point by the Opposition who asserted, first, that the Act of 1909 had worked satisfactorily and that no unnecessary delays had resulted from the Provisional Order system; [45] second, that no reason was given by the Govern-

although it was provided that they could be annulled within forty days by Parliament (Clause 2, sub-section (4)). It was said that the Bill gave the Minister "absolute personal and automatic volition" (107 H. C. Deb. 5 s. 90), that it "is setting up a Ministry and a very new Ministry, absolutely with authority over the authority of this House" (107 H. C. Deb. 5 s. 91), that the new procedure was not a democratic principle (108 H. C. Deb. 5 s. 1492), and that it gave the Minister "carte blanche" (108 H. C. Deb. 5 s. 1508). One member, moreover, did not like the idea "that we as Members of this House should abrogate all our powers." 108 H. C. Debt. 5 s. 1502.

[43] 107 H. C. Deb. 5 s. 121. Mr. G. Roberts, the Minister of Labour, said: "Under the Standing Orders of the House no Bill for this confirmation of a provisional Order may be read the first time after Whitsuntide, and the House of Lords usually directs by a Sessional Order that no such Bill brought from the Commons may be read a second time after a fixed date in June.... But, assuming [that these conditions were met] a period of about three months would usually elapse between the First Reading and the securing of the Royal Assent.... In the event of a Bill being opposed, there seems to be almost unlimited opportunities of obstructing its passage." Thus, he added, the Provisional Order system was "cumbrous and dilatory". 108 H. C. Deb. 5 s. 1488-9.

[44] Mr. Roberts said: "The substitution of procedure by Special Order for that by Provisional Order does not withdraw the control of Parliament over the application of the Act to new trades. It seems to me and to those with whom I act that this is an ample safeguard, and that, therefore, the proposal is not open to the dangerous conjecture suggested in some of the criticisms that have been made." 107 H. C. Deb. 5 s. 64.

[45] "Experience of this Act [of 1909] shows that that procedure [of Provisional Order] does not in the least prevent the speedy passing of the law." 107 H. C. Deb. 5 s. 80. The Minister of Labour, moreover,

ment for the proposed change;[46] and, last, that the safeguard of laying the Orders on the Table for forty days was hardly enough to secure any degree of parliamentary control.[47]

It is evident that the questions raised by the controversy on the Provisional and Special Order systems were of a nature to defy conclusive answer. The answer to the question, for instance, whether the Trade Boards Act, 1909, had worked satisfactorily depended in large measure on the extent to which the aims of individual members were achieved. One member cited the laundry trade as "a trade which was crying out for inclusion in the Trade Boards Bill"; he found, however, that its applications for Provisional Orders were unsuccessful because of the opposition of other powerful interests to its inclusion in the Act.[48] The Special Order system would have resulted more favorably. The instance

"gave no example to show that the provision in the Act of 1909 had not operated quite successfully." 107 H. C. Deb. 5 s. 81. "There has been," asserted another member, "in the past nine years no difficulty whatever in bringing other trades under the Trade Boards Act, where the Government has desired it." 107 H. C. Deb. 5 s. 116.

[46] "The Bill of 1909," said one member, "was made to work through the machinery of Provisional Orders, which gave an opportunity to anyone who objected to the proposals to be heard, and an opportunity for this House to keep control over the matter, because those Provisional Orders had to be confirmed by Parliament. Has a case been made out for abandoning those safeguards?" 107 H. C. Deb. 5 s. 74. Sir Frederick Banbury likewise declared that the Minister of Labour failed to give the House an adequate reason why the old procedure should be departed from. 107 H. C. Deb. 5 s. 109.

[47] Mr. J. Mason expressed the fear that the Government might present the Special Orders on "the day before the Summer Recess, and the whole forty days would be passed before the House met again to consider them. There is no provision saying forty working days, but only that they shall lay on the Table of the House for forty days." 107 H. C. Deb. 5 s. 75. Sir Frederick Banbury thought that the forty days were an "absolutely illusory" safeguard on account of the Rules of the House of Commons. 107 H. S. Deb. 5 s. 110.

[48] 107 H. C. Deb. 5 s. 90.

cited was challenged by others as exceptional.[49] Again, agreement was hardly possible upon the adequacy of the forty-day safeguard because the disputants were not in agreement as to the ends to be achieved. The executive's view of parliamentary control could scarcely prove acceptable to a thorough-going opponent of delegation.[50]

So much for the Provisional and Special Order controversy. The debate in the Trade Boards Act, 1909, turned on no technical question, and did not involve a mere attempt to evaluate the efficiency of different methods of control. It was parliamentary control, itself, that was conceived to be at stake.

Another safeguard frequently advocated was the provision that the regulations issued by the executive should not be operative until approved by Parliament, or should not be operative beyond a specified period unless approved by resolution within that time. Mr. Percy Harris, in the debate on the London Traffic Act, 1924, moved an amendment of that nature,[51] which the Government characterized as " much too complicated " and " positively mischievous ".[52] A number of speeches were made in favor of the proposal, one of which was an appeal to the back-benchers to assert their rights against the encroachments of the front bench.[53] The amendment was carried despite the Government's opposition. The Lords yielded little to the Commons in the violence of

[49] 107 H. C. Deb. 5 s. 116.

[50] While Mr. G. Roberts, the Minister of Labour, called the proposed safeguard of forty days "an ample safeguard", the Opposition saw in it a removal of parliamentary control and no safeguard at all. 107 H. C. Deb. 5 s. 64 and 77.

[51] 175 H. C. Deb. 5 s. 383-4. It should be noted that the amendment provided for a resolution in the House of Commons alone.

[52] 175 H. C. Deb. 5 s. 385.

[53] "This is not a question as between Liberals and Conservatives or Liberals and Labour Members, or Socialists, but it is a question of back bench against front bench." 175 H. C. Deb. 5 s. 388.

the denunciations of delegation and demands for more effective safeguards were repeatedly made; [54] the Clause which had been amended by the Commons to require an affirmative resolution in the House of Commons before an Order could take effect was, however, restored to its original form by the Lords, i. e., to lie twenty-one days on the Tables of both Houses.[55] An amendment of the same nature was moved to the Board of Guardians Act, 1926. This amendment, as one member said, was designed "to put every impediment in the way of the unrestrained use of power by the Minister of Health" and "to provide full opportunities for discussion." [56] "Parliament", it was said, "should at least reserve that power to itself." [57]

In the vigorous debate on the Local Government Act, 1929, Mr. Atkinson moved an amendment providing that regulations purporting to amend the Act must receive the specific sanction of both Houses of Parliament in order to become effective. One of the supporters of the amendment urged that it would remove "the theoretical objection which many of us feel to the clause [Clause 111], in its present form" which followed "a recent bad tradition" and represented a "departure from sound constitutional principle." [58] Mr. Atkinson, speaking in support of the amendment which he had moved, contended that, failing adoption of the amendment, Parliament would be unable, when in recess, to check the Government despite its right to annul the Orders when

[54] E. g. 58 H. L. Deb. 5 s. 811, 879-880, 882 *et seq.*

[55] 58 H. L. Deb. 5 s. 885 *et seq.*

[56] 197 H. C. Deb. 5 s. 2425.

[57] 197 H. C. Deb. 5 s. 2426.

[58] 224 H. C. Deb. 5 s. 971. It is interesting to note that three amendments were proposed to this Clause. Sir Henry Slesser said: "All these Amendments are moved, I think, by students or practitioners of the law. It is a matter of pride to us that the lawyers in this House are the guardians of our liberties." 224 H. C. Deb. 5 s. 976.

in session.[59] Moreover, such a resolution could " take place in the course of an evening " so that no question of emergency would be involved.[60] In the House of Lords Earl Russell supported an amendment of the same purport. He stressed the fact that whereas the Rules of the House of Lords did not prevent effective use of the negative safeguards from being made, the procedural rigors of the Commons often would not permit a private member to challenge Orders laid on the Table.[61] The Lord Chancellor, however, would not accept the amendment, but moved a compromise scheme

[59] If orders were issued during a parliamentary recess, Parliament " cannot undo what has been done. Therefore it (*sic*) an Order has been made which has repealed or varied some of the provisions of the Act, and has been acted upon, the House has no means of putting that right. They can only put it right by passing another Act of Parliament, which would have to be retrospective, a proceeding which is always open to objection." He continued: " As a matter of principle, are we, if a difficulty arise in carrying out any legislation when the House is not sitting, going to delegate the legislative powers of the House to some Minister? ... This is a very dangerous principle, and one cannot quite see why or how a difficulty might arise which demands such immediate relief or attention that it cannot wait until the House sits again ... the House seems to be always sitting for the great part of the year, and the small objection to the postponement of the decision of the House for a few weeks cannot outweigh the very serious objections to setting up the precedent of permitting a Minister to have such wide powers as include an unlimited modification of almost every provision in the Bill without the House retaining control." 225 H. C. Deb. 5 s. 636-8.

[60] 225 H. C. Deb. 5 s. 637.

[61] Lord Russell said in part: " In your Lordships' House no difficulty will arise from a merely negative Resolution being required, because no one would have any difficulty in raising a debate upon it, and, if he could, in carrying a negative Resolution. But your Lordships know very well that in another place that is not so. It would be impossible in another place for a private Member who wanted to challenge one of the Orders to find or obtain time or opportunity to move a negative Resolution before the Order became effective. It is in order that he should be given an opportunity of challenging an Order that I suggest that an affirmative Resolution would be a better manner of dealing with it." 72 H. L. Deb. 5 s. 1139.

which was carried and later accepted by the House of Commons.[62]

Still another safeguard demanded by members of Parliament was the establishment of a committee of one or both Houses to scrutinize the rules and orders issued by the departments under statutory authority. Sir John Marriott, on February 25, 1929, addressed a question to Prime Minister Baldwin asking him "whether he is prepared to propose to Parliament the setting up of a Sessional Joint Committee to scrutinize all Statutory Rules and Orders issued by His Majesty's Privy Council or by public Departments and, if deemed necessary by the Committee, to report thereon to Parliament."[63] The Prime Minister was non-committal in his answer. Lord Hundson of Hundson, in the debate on the Local Government Act, 1929, likewise moved an amendment that an Order issued by the Minister of Health "shall not be of any effect unless and until the Order is approved by a committee to be appointed by Parliament, or, failing that approval, unless and until a Resolution affirming the Order is passed by each House of Parliament."[64] The amendment,

[62] The original Clause provided that "Every Order made under this section shall be laid before Parliament as soon as may be after it is made." The Lord Chancellor's amendment provided "for an affirmative Resolution to be carried within three months after Parliament first met after the date when an Order was made." 73 H. L. Deb. 5 s. 609-610. This was in line with the suggestion of Earl Beauchamp who said: "To say that the Order shall lie upon the Table of the House for some unlimited period does not seem to me to give to either House quite the same authority as if there was a definite period fixed in the Bill during which it is to lie upon the Table." 72 H. L. Deb. 5 s. 1100-1. Sir A. Hopkinson, in the Commons, expressed his approval of the Lords' amendment in these words: "The other place has secured a very happy solution. The Minister can act and can act at once, and the beauty of it is that his act, though it comes into operation at once, as was absolutely necessary, is to be limited in time until this House has had the opportunity of confirming it." 226 H. C. Deb. 5 s. 2032.

[63] 225 H. C. Deb. 5 s. 1564-5.

[64] 73 H. L. Deb. 5 s. 379.

however, was not accepted by the Government and was subsequently withdrawn.

Throughout the *Parliamentary Debates* may be found demands upon the Ministers for assurances that the delegated power will not be exercised in ways contrary to Parliament's intentions. For instance, the Minister was asked to give "assurance that that power shall not be used in an autocratic way."[65] Again, members demanded that the Minister should promise to provide an opportunity for proper discussion of the Statutory Rules and Orders in the House.[66] Fearing that bad precedents might lead to worse practices later, some members asked the Ministers to agree that the particular Bill under discussion should not constitute a precedent for the future.[67] Such promises and pledges were given more or less freely by the Treasury Bench.

It is interesting to note that while Parliament had been very energetic in its demand for a more effective parliamentary safeguard, it had more or less ignored the two other forms of safeguards: the administrative and the judicial. When the Rules Publication Act, 1893, was under discussion, Parliament raised no questtion about its provisions. In fact, the Bill was not debated because it was said to have received the approval of all the Government departments. There were, however, occasional complaints in Parliament, expressed in the form of questions, with regard to certain Statutory Rules and Orders which failed to appear, or appeared too late, in the *London Gazette*.[68] During debates on some

[65] 175 H. C. Deb. 5 s. 344 (London Traffic Act, 1924).

[66] 259 H. C. Deb. 5 s. 1092-3 (The Abnormal Importations (Customs Duties) Act. 1931).

[67] 260 H. C. Deb. 5 s. 1739-40.

[68] Mr. Gilbert, in a question on August 4, 1921, complained that draft Statutory Rules and Orders, to which Section 1 of the Rules Publication Act, 1893, applied, were often not obtainable in the London *Gazette*; and, "in view of the great and growing importance of the legislation under

Bills, moreover, publicity and the holding of public inquiries were sometimes demanded and almost always promised.[69] For the judicial safeguard, Parliament, unlike the publicists and writers, showed very little concern. Although Prime Minister Baldwin, in his answer to a question of Sir John Marriott, defined the judicial safeguard in no uncertain terms,[70] Sir John was inclined to cast doubt upon the value of this safeguard, characterizing it as "utterly inadequate and illusory".[71] Except for one or two other passing remarks, the judicial safeguard was not discussed in Parliament. The frequent allusions to the Courts of law in *Hansard* are principally concerned with the delegation of judicial powers, a subject which has also exercised the members of Parliament very much.

Statutory authority by Order in Council and Government Departments", the Chancellor of the Exchequer should make arrangements for their prompt publication. 145 H. C. Deb. 5 s. 1665-6. Commander Bellaires asked a supplementary question on March 4, 1929, saying that some Orders could not be found in the London *Gazette*. Prime Minister Baldwin answered by saying that it was not his habit to read the London *Gazette*. 226 H. C. Deb. 5 s. 25.

[69] Mr. H. H. Fowler, the President of the Local Government Board who introduced the Local Government Act, 1894, gave the following assurance: "When I induced the House to grant to the Local Government Board powers which were considered very doubtful by many hon. Members—that is to say, powers which had hitherto been exercised by Parliament alone, it was upon a distinct understanding that the Local Government Board should hold an inquiry in every case." 20 *Hansard*, 4 s. 910. Mr. G. Roberts, the Minister of Labour in charge of the Trade Boards Act, 1918, said that the Special Order procedure "assures full publicity and ample opportunity for inquiry and for the ventilation of any grievances." 108 H. C. Deb. 5 s. 1491. The Ministry of Transport Act, 1919, was the occasion for the assertion by one member that "we want as much publicity as possible, and the whole policy of the Government and Parliament ought to be to give as much publicity as possible to what they are doing." 117 H. C. Deb. 5 s. 861. These are but a few of the numerous examples of this demand for publicity and public inquiry.

[70] 225 H. C. Deb. 5 s. 1564.

[71] 226 H. C. Deb. 5 s. 2511.

CHAPTER V

Justification of Delegated Legislation

Our conception of democracy is identical with the conception of Sir William Anson . . . that democracy has the right to delegate its powers if it thinks proper.

Mr. Hore-Belisha in 259 H. C. Deb. 5 s. 780.

Administrative discretion is of the essence of the modern State.

Harold J. Laski.

Despite the parliamentary wails which we have recorded in the preceding two chapters, delegated legislation must gain in momentum as the field of legislation widens and as more and more emergency situations confront the British government. Although the practice may have done violence to some of the fundamental principles of the British constitution as the " watch-dogs " or " guardians " of the constitution allege, there are many reasons which show that the practice is an inevitable one and that the constitution has not been violated as has been said. The present chapter will summarize the chief reasons and arguments which the Ministers and their supporters give when they answer the charges of the critics in the Houses of Parliament.

The chief reason for the delegation of legislative powers is the pressure of parliamentary business. The economical use of parliamentary time and the relief of " parliamentary congestion " are the points most frequently made in support of such delegation. The physical circumstance is more compelling than all the arguments in *Hansard*.

Thus, when the system of Orders in Council was advocated for the Local Government Act, 1888, one of the reasons in its favor was that it would enable Parliament to avoid the waste of time which would result if the transfer of powers to the County Councils should be effected by provisions in the Schedules of the Act.[1] The Special Order system was urged for the Trade Boards Act, 1918, in lieu of the Provisional Order system employed by the Trade Boards Act, 1909, because of

> the congested state of Parliament. . . . After the War, undoubtedly Imperial and domestic questions will emerge with great rapidity, and it does seem desirable that where it is possible to delegate to responsible bodies matters which would otherwise occupy Parliamentary time, that is very wise and expedient.[2]

As was shown in the first chapter, modern statutes, as contrasted with statutes in the past, are much longer, more complicated and technical in spite of the fact that many gaps and details are left to be filled by the Government departments. The complicated and technical nature of these statutes is a good reason for delegating wide regulatory powers to the specialists and experts who make up the highly professionalized staffs of the departments. The complicated and technical nature of modern statutes also gives rise to difficulties in their daily application which cannot be foreseen and provided for in the Acts themselves. Powers should, therefore, be delegated to the departments to handle these contingencies so that they can be met easily and quickly.

Lord Althorp, in the debate on the Poor Law Act, 1834, contended that " it would be utterly impossible to carry any improvement in the present system of Poor-Laws into effect without acting upon great discretionary powers." [3] Mr. Rit-

[1] 327 *Hansard*, 3 s. 631-2. But Mr. Channing was willing to spend " several weeks longer, if necessary, to carry out the only sound principle that these matters should be dealt with in Parliament." 327 *Hansard*, 3 s. 641.

[2] 107 H. C. Deb. 5 s. 64 (Mr. G. Roberts, the Minister of Labour).

[3] 22 *Hansard*, 3 s. 883.

chie, introducing the Local Government Act, 1888, pointed out the complications that were involved in the Bill and urged that they should be left to the experts in the Local Government Board or to investigating committees to be appointed by the Board.[4] The National Insurance Act, 1911, involved a highly contentious principle so that, after discussing it, Parliament could not possibly find enough time to give the Bill's long and technical clauses detailed consideration. It was therefore natural that the Ministers in charge should have justified the provisions delegating legislative powers by pointing out these characteristics of the Bill, an argument which was not lost upon the members. Thus Sir T. Whittaker believed that "if we are to go on discussing details of great measures in this House we will not be able to get on at all" because "an Assembly of 670 Members, with two or three hundred in daily attendance, is not at all suited for the discussion of the minute details of a measure like this."[5] Mr. McKenna, the Home Secretary, made the further point that "it is inevitable some matters may have been overlooked. Some authority ought to have the power to set the machinery at work."[6] The same argument was exploited by Sir Kingsley Wood in the debate on the Rating and Valuation Act, 1925, in justification of the "Power to modify local Acts" clause,[7] and by one member in the debate on the Local Government Act, 1929, when the "Henry VIII" clause was under discussion.[8] In the same

[4] 328 *Hansard*, 3 s. 1280.

[5] 32 H. C. Deb. 5 s. 1479.

[6] 30 H. C. Deb. 5 s. 2009.

[7] Sir Kingsley said: "Obviously, in connection with a complicated Bill of this kind, there must be some Clause of this character giving the Minister this particular power." 188 H. C. Deb. 5 s. 1900.

[8] "When you come to consider the question of such a large, important, technical, and in some respects complicated Bill as that which we are now discussing, it is inevitable that as soon as a far-reaching scheme of

vein, Mr. Neville Chamberlain answered the charges of the Opposition by saying that more powers should be delegated to the Ministry of Health by the Local Government Act, 1929, than by other Acts for the simple reason that the Act was more complicated.[9]

Closely akin to this argument on the complicated and technical nature of modern statutes is the plea for uniformity, elasticity, and efficiency in public administration. This cannot be achieved by parliamentary legislation because any comprehensive legislative endeavor would involve a comprehensive survey of the whole field, a thing which Parliament cannot accomplish within the time at its command. As long ago as 1834, Lord Althorp, the Minister in charge of the Poor Law Act of that year, advanced the argument that the investment of wide discretionary powers in the hands of Poor Law Commissioners had for its object the attainment of "an uniformity of system throughout the country." [10] The complaints against the Prison Acts of 1865 and 1877 were that the rules and regulations embodied in the Schedules of the Acts could not be modified by prison administrators to meet individual cases so that because of the cruelty and inhumanity of the treatment of prisoners in exceptional circumstances the whole system of prison administration had been discredited. The Bill of 1898 was designed to remedy this evil by transferring the rule-making power from Parliament to the Home Department in order to vest the Secretary with power to take care of individual cases as they came up. In other words, the whole change proposed

this description is put into effect some unforeseen contingencies must arise at the outset which require to be speedily dealt with if they are to be nipped in the bud before the consequences have become too serious. Such a Clause, in such circumstances, is, in my view, not only desirable, but almost necessary." 225 H. C. Deb. 5 s. 890-1.

[9] 225 H. C. Deb. 5 s. 595.

[10] 22 *Hansard*, 3 s. 883.

had for its object the achievement of elasticity in prison rules and regulations.[11] Similarly, Mr. John Burns, in charge of the Housing Act, 1909, justified the Departmental Order system on the ground that [12]

> it dispenses with confirmation by Parliament, and we can apply the order at any time without waiting for Parliament to assemble, and therefore it makes for promptitude in meeting the demands of the local authority.

Similarly, during the debate on the Import Duties Act, 1932, Mr. Neville Chamberlain, the Chancellor of the Exchequer of the "National Government", justified the delegation of wide powers to the Treasury, the Board of Trade and the Import Duties Advisory Committee on the ground that the exigency of the economic crisis demanded elasticity and flexibility.[13]

Parliament is not in session all year round. Events may happen during a parliamentary recess which demand immediate regulation. The Ministers enjoy no stated vacations.

[11] Sir M. W. Ridley, the Home Secretary, remarked: "I think the fault which is to be found with our prison system ... is its want of elasticity, by which ... I mean there is a vast number of statutory rules which cannot be dispensed with, and there is a lack of power for the individual treatment of cases." 55 *Hansard,* 4 s. 836.

[12] 10 H. C. Deb. 5 s. 62.

[13] Mr. Chamberlain said in part: "What we have to seek for is a plan which will be flexible and elastic, a plan which can readily be varied and adapted to suit changing conditions, a plan which will allow, first one element and then another element, to come forward according as the balance of advantage lies on this side or that." 261 H. C. Deb. 5 s. 286. Major Elliot, speaking for the Government, said: "The powers of the Treasury to alter a duty so that it may be changed, 'by reference to value, to weight, to measurement or to quantity', are set out with a view of providing the utmost flexibility to the machinery which we propose to adopt, because we recognise that we are here in an experimental period and dealing with a difficulty which no other nation has ever had to face." 261 H. C. Deb. 5 s. 384.

Therefore, in order to meet extraordinary circumstances the Ministers should be given power to legislate for these contingencies, not only during a parliamentary recess but in the midst of parliamentary sessions as well. Such was the argument advanced by Mr. Neville Chamberlain in the debate on the Board of Guardians Act, 1926; and such was the reason which he urged in support of Clause 86 of the Local Government Act, 1929.[14] What is more important, Mr. Chamberlain expressly pointed out that even if his Orders met with parliamentary disapproval when they came up, "nevertheless that is without prejudice to anything which may have been done under the Order as long as it had been in force." [15] Nothing is better calculated to defeat the purposes of a safeguard than this frank confession of Mr. Chamberlain.

All these demands for "uniformity", "elasticity" and "promptitude" were made in the name of governmental efficiency in times of normal national life. But there are periods in the history of a nation when grave crises threaten the very existence of the State and the life of the people. It behooves the government to meet these crises: and past Governments have never shirked this heavy responsibility.

[14] On the former Bill, Mr. Chamberlain said: "We are not sitting all the year round, and supposing the emergency for an Order arises when the House is not sitting, it would be impossible to do anything, and you might get a complete stoppage." It is of interest to note that this was the chief reason which he gave in refutation of the arguments advanced by twelve successive speeches in support of an amendment providing for an affirmative resolution before an Order took effect. The Division Lobbies, as might have been expected, defeated the amendment in accordance with the party alignment. 197 H. C. Deb. 5 s. 2442. On the latter Bill, he made substantially the same remarks. "There might be a deadlock and something must be done at once. You could not wait until Parliament has passed a resolution; Parliament might not be in Session at the tme." Hence Clause 86. 224 H. C. Deb. 5 s. 977.

[15] 197 H. C. Deb. 5 s. 2442.

In fact, "emergency legislation", according to Prime Minister MacDonald,[16]

> has characterized the whole history of Parliamentary government in this country. First one emergency and then another has had to be dealt with, not by maintaining the normal procedure of the House of Commons, for the simple reason that the House of Commons, in the circumstances, could not maintain its normal procedure.

It had long since become the practice to meet such abnormal or extraordinary situations by exalting the executive at the expense of the legislature: at first legislative powers had been delegated to the Privy Council and later to the various Government departments. The history of delegated legislation abounds with examples of legislation for this purpose,[17] ranging all the way from the prevention of diseases of animals and plants to the achievement of victory in a world war. The Cholera Act, 1832, had for its purpose the employment of extraordinary measures to prevent the spread of this deadly disease as well as to relieve and bury the victims. These extraordinary measures could not await

[16] 256 H. C. Deb. 5 s. 419 (The National Economy Act, 1931).

[17] Mr. Cecil T. Carr thinks that the handling of crises is the greatest justification of delegated legislation. *Delegated Legislation* (Cambridge, 1921), p. 21. Professor F. J. Port admonishes his readers to "remember ... that Parliament is not always in session, and also that its processes are slow and unwieldy. The administrative function must be ready at any moment to meet a crisis . . . and as far as possible the legislature must give the Government wide powers to lay down such general rules as are necessary to ensure the national well-being." *Administrative Law* (London, 1929), p. 137. A general discussion of the emergency measures which had been passed by Parliament granting extraordinary powers to the Government of the day is contained in these treatises. It is of interest to note that one of the earliest examples of delegated legislation is an emergency measure. It is the Statute of Proclamations, 1539, which was passed for the express purpose of meeting "sodden causes and occasions fortune many tymes do require spedy remedyes."

the consent of Parliament with its procedural niceties.[18] The reasons given by Lord Althorp for such an extravagant request for discretionary powers were as follows:[19]

Although orders in Council might be issued, yet there was no power, as the law at present stood, to carry those orders into effect, and, therefore, the necessary regulations for the purpose of preventing contagion . . . could not be efficiently made in the present state of the law.

This model, minus references to the Deity, was later copied in coping with various other diseases, human, animal and plant alike.[20] An investigation of the debates on these various emergency measures shows that Parliament was quite willing to delegate its legislative powers where a case of emergency was proved to exist.[21] Parliament was inclined

[18] The Preamble of this Act reads: "Whereas it has pleased Almighty God to visit the United Kingdom with the disease called the cholera or spasmodic or Indian cholera, and whereas, with a view to prevent as far as may be possible by the Divine Blessing the spreading of the said disease, it may be necessary that rules and regulations may from time to time be established within cities, towns or districts affected with or which may be threatened by the said disease, but it may be impossible to establish such rules and regulations by the authority of Parliament with sufficient promptitude to meet the exigency of any such case as it may occur."

[19] 10 *Hansard*, 3 s. 337.

[20] In 1847 the method applied against cholera in 1832 was extended to other diseases. In 1848 a similar power was delegated under the first of a series of Diseases of Animals Acts. In 1877 its use was extended to "destructive insects and pests" in the vegetable kingdom. In 1858 the Privy Council was authorized to make regulations for the efficient performance of vaccination. In 1889 the power was given to make orders for the muzzling of dogs. The spread of all these diseases and the preventive measures to be taken were all considered as grave emergencies and therefore justified extraordinary treatment.

[21] The Bills for the prevention and treatment of all these diseases were generally passed without much adverse criticism by Parliament. Thus, the Cholera Act, 1832, was received enthusiastically by the two Houses. Some objections were raised against the Public Health Act,

to let the measures pass without question when the Government made the plea of emergency.

The greatest national crisis that Great Britain has had to meet in modern times was undoubtedly the World War. Nor did its termination result in any let-up. From the commencement of the War in 1914 up to the present day, England has been faced with one emergency after another. To meet the situation, her Government resorted to emergency laws. Almost immediately after the outbreak of hostilities, Parliament rushed through the Defense of the Realm Acts, vesting in the Government unprecedented powers to make rules and regulations for national defense; the effects of some of the rules issued under the authority of these Acts are still felt at the present time.[22] In the midst of great excitement and intense anxiety the first D. O. R. A.

1848, but these were chiefly directed against the newly created sanitary districts. That there was no objection to the delegation of discretionary powers was shown when one member made it known that he preferred the form of the Cholera Act, 1832, to that of the pending Bill. (The Act of 1848 created sanitary districts which were at variance both with the Poor Law districts and the Highway districts constituted in 1835. This new arrangement was challenged as a measure of centralization and as placing tremendous powers in the hands of the executive to distribute patronage. See 98 *Hansard*, 3 s. 712 and 792. Mr. Frewen preferred the model of 1832. 98 *Hansard*, 3 s. 813.) The prevention of the introduction and spread of the "Colorado beetle" by vesting rule-making powers in the Privy Council provoked no criticism when the Government made good its claim of urgency. See 236 *Hansard*, 3 s. 780, 598-9. The same was true of the Diseases of Animals Act, 1894. See 28 *Hansard*, 4 s. 1077. The Destructive Insects and Pest Act, 1907, which was an extension of that of 1877, was not contested at all. 174 *Hansard*, 4 s.

[22] These Defense of the Realm Acts were nicknamed 'DORA' after the first letters of the words of the short-title. There are at present some individuals who organized a movement for the purpose of eliminating from the Statute Book some of the obnoxious rules which still remain there. Somewhat humorously, they have taken over the name 'DORA" as a short-hand expression for the "Defense of Rights and Amusements". *The New York Times*, June 19, 1932.

went through its parliamentary stages substantially without debate.[23] The Government did not have to prove the desperateness of the situation, for it needed no proof. The Defense of the Realm (Amendment) Act provoked some discussion because its provisions for the suspension of trial by jury and for the institution of martial law were considered by some members as violating the basic British constitutional principles. But the Government was of the opinion that that was "no time to indulge in general heroics", and that so long as these Acts were necessary, the argument that "they are novel and do violence to our constitutional traditions is an argument of very little weight." [24]

Two years after the Armistice, the Coalition Government proposed to continue some of the laws enacted during the crisis.[25] The Government considered that the War, though terminated on the battlefields, had brought in its train disturbing conditions which must be treated as urgent. Among them, the most threatening was the strikes which might paralyze the economic life of the nation. The Government introduced the Emergency Powers Act, 1920, in an attempt to forestall a major national crisis. Whatever the theoretical possibility of damage to the British constitution, the Government, in view of the desperate situation, must be armed with powers "to deal with the situation as it arises." [26] A storm of protests from members of Parliament followed,

[23] There are instances in which a Bill passes through all its stages in a single day, e. g., the Explosives Act, 1883, and the Postponement of Payments Act, 1914. *Cf.* Lindsay Rogers, "The War and the British Constitution", *The Forum*, July, 1915.

[24] 70 H. C. Deb. 5 s. 299 and 289.

[25] The War Emergency Laws (Continuation) Act, 1920.

[26] Bonar Law in 133 H. C. Deb. 5 s. 1401.

but the Government regarded the grant as an absolute necessity if the needs of the time were to be met.[27]

The economic depression which began in 1930 caused Great Britain to form "the National Government" described by a Scottish member as "a mixsey-maksey hotch-potch." [28] This Government, headed by Mr. Ramsay MacDonald, sought to meet the situation by a series of six laws,[29] which delegated wide and extensive legislative and regulatory powers to the Government departments and the Privy Council. The *raison d'etre* for these broad grants of discretionary powers was the economic crisis: they were compared to the Defense of the Realm Acts [30] and the Emergency Powers Act.[31] According to one member, on the question whether the parliamentary form of government could weather the storm and stress of national emergency depended the question whether it was fit to govern a modern State.[32] "The functions of democracy", according to another member,[33]

> need in no way be impinged upon if the executive is equipped with considerable additional powers in order to take rapid and effective action especially in times of crisis. I think that is

[27] Protests may be found in 133 H. C. Deb. 5 s. 1419, 1421-2, 1430, 1592, 1602, 1651, 1699, 1798, 1805, 1808, 1819, 1826-7, and 1839.

[28] 259 H. C. Deb. 5 s. 812.

[29] They are: The Gold Standard (Amendment) Act, The National Economy Act, The Foodstuffs (Prevention of Exploitation) Act, The Abnormal Importations (Customs Duties) Act, and The Horticultural Products (Emergency Custom Duties) Act, all of 1931, and The Imports Duties Act, 1932.

[30] 256 H. C. Deb. 5 s. 637.

[31] 257 H. C. Deb. 5 s. 1012.

[32] Mr. MacDonald in 256 H. C. Deb. 5 s. 419. Captain Fraser made the same point when he said: "If the House of Commons was not competent to adapt itself to the needs of special circumstances, it would not be competent to serve the nation at all." 259 H. C. Deb. 5 s. 813.

[33] Mr. Boothby in 256 H. C. Deb. 5 s. 573.

inevitable in view of the complex nature of the problems which confront us and the speed at which we live—a speed far greater than that of earlier times.

Finally, the " National Government " was returned to meet an emergency. They must be given " authority to act with unfettered discretion." [34] " The House ", as Major Elliot said,[35]

> was elected by a great majority to give discretion to the Executive so far as possible to deal with the circumstances of the time. This is an exceptional Parliament. It is not the Executive which is asking for this discretion, but the Government of the day, and it is the Government of the day that this Parliament by an overwhelming majority was elected to support, *and not merely to support, but to authorise it to demand a free hand to deal with this emergency.*

The six measures were put on the Statute Book by means of what are called " mechanical majorities ",[36] though under the constant fire of a diminutive but determined Opposition.

Thus far we have concerned ourselves with reasons for delegated legislation which may be regarded as inherent in the present British constitutional system as they were voiced by members of Parliament, especially those on the Treasury Bench, during the debates on the various Bills delegating

[34] Mr. Runciman in 261 H. C. Deb. 5 s. 691.

[35] 262 H. C. Deb. 5 s. 289. Italics mine. *Cf.* remarks of Mr. Albery who replied: " Unfortunately, powers which are taken in times of emergency only too frequently become powers which are subsequently taken as a matter of custom." 262 H. C. Deb. 5 s. 289.

[36] The futility of opposition was more than once pointed out by members in the debates on these Bills. E. g. Mr. Baty said: " Although when we go into the Lobbies the decision may be a foregone conclusion the Opposition are justified in registering their disapproval of this revolutionary method." 259 H. C. Deb. 5 s. 1084. *Cf.* remarks of Mr. Bevan in 259 H. C. Deb. 5 s. 1092.

legislative powers to the executive. These new strains on the British constitutional structure have to be eased by novel methods of which delegated legislation is but one. In fact, in the opinion of one member at least, the burden of making rules and regulations was frequently thrust upon the Government because of sheer necessity and against their wishes.[37] Whether thrust upon them or not, the apologists never failed to use these facts as arguments in justification of their demands for powers.

In addition to the arguments just recited, the Government has employed many others which are not occasioned by the requirements of the new age but which are simply arguments in answer to those advanced by the critics of delegated legislation. Three of these are of prime importance and deserve attention: they are the appeal to precedents, the responsibility of rule-making authorities to the House of Commons, and the history of the exercise of powers formerly delegated. They will be treated in the order given.

In view of the important part which precedents have played in English legal development, it is only natural that the apologists of delegated legislation should cite past examples to justify their case. They could point to provision after provision which previous Parliaments had found acceptable. The expansion of the executive's activity into new fields made it difficult, however, to write the provisions of old statutes into pending legislation *verbatim et literatim*. For this reason Ministers could constantly be challenged to demonstrate the justness of the analogies offered. The critics of delegated legislation were not loath to dispute and question the propriety of the precedents invoked; the refine-

[37] Colonel Ashley, in the debate on the Road Transport Lighting Act, 1927, said: "I wish to put this to the House, that a Minister does not really desire these Regulations because he wants power to be able to do things, but very often they are put upon him because there is no other way of arriving at the desired object." 204 H. C. Deb. 5 s. 1615.

ments of legal casuistry were attentuated to a microscopic hairline in the struggle to distinguish the cases.

As long ago as 1834, Lord Althorp defended the Poor Law Act of that year by saying that "there were some Acts of Parliament and many local Acts which conferred as great powers as this Bill did", although he failed to supply the specific instance.[38] Mr. Gladstone found that "the course taken by the Government" in the Endowed Schools Act, 1869, "was in accordance with both precedent and reason."[39] The Factory and Workshops Acts Amendment Act, 1901, was justified by the Act of 1895.[40] The Housing Act of 1909 was justified by that of 1907.[41] Two previous Acts were cited as precedents for the National Insurance Act, 1911.[42] The Trade Boards Act, 1918, was said to follow generally the precedent set by the Factory and Workshop Act, 1901.[43] There were precedents for the Roads Act, 1920, and for the London Traffic Act, 1924.[44] The Education Act, 1902, was the model for the Rating and Valuation Act, 1925.[45] The Earl of Onslow enumerated a series of statutes to prove that "there is nothing new in the principle of" the Board of Guardians Act, 1926.[46] The prin-

[38] 23 *Hansard*, 3 s. 983.

[39] 196 *Hansard*, 3 s. 1747.

[40] 95 *Hansard*, 4 s. 125.

[41] 10 H. C. Deb. 5 s. 193.

[42] Mr. Lloyd George cited the Local Government Act, 1888, and Sir T. Whittaker cited the Licensing Act, 1904. See 30 H. C. Deb. 5 s. 187 and 32 H. C. Deb. 5 s. 1479. In answer to a question, Mr. Lloyd George asserted that "in every Act of Parliament, certainly (*sic*) which has been passed in the last 10 or 15 years, there have always been provisions of this kind for framing regulations ... it was common form in almost every Act." 26 H. C. Deb. 5 s. 710-1.

[43] 107 H. C. Deb. 5 s. 64.

[44] 135 H. C. Deb. 5 s. 1527.

[45] 175 H. C. Deb. 5 s. 281.

[46] 68 H. L. Deb. 5 s. 151.

cipal argument which Mr. Neville Chamberlain used in defending the Local Government Act, 1929, was the citation of six statutes as precedents for the Bill.[47] "What we are proposing to do", he said, "has behind it a great weight of examples from other Acts of Parliament passed by this or preceding Governments."[48] The same argument was employed by the Lord Chancellor in the House of Lords.[49] As has been noted above, the group of five Acts passed in 1931 to meet the economic crisis were compared to the Defense of the Realm Acts and the Emergency Powers Act.[50]

This citation of precedents, however, seldom went without challenge.[51] The difficulty of copying word for word from previous statutes gives to the critics of delegated legislation the chance to consider the precedents as "inadequate" and "irrelevant".[52] Other members took the line that though the precedents adduced might be in point there was no reason to follow bad examples, especially since the process had a habit of leading from bad to worse.[53] Many a bad precedent had been overruled by subsequent decisions in the courts of law where precedents are highly respected; there was no reason why a bad method of legislation should not in like manner be abolished.

[47] Mr. Chamberlain cited as precedents for Section 130, Section 108 of the Local Government Act, 1888, Section 80 of the Local Government Act, 1894, Section 78 of the National Insurance Act, 1911, Section 45 of the Unemployment Insurance Act, 1920, Section 35 of the Widows', Orphans', and Old Age Contributory Pensions Act, 1925, and Section 67 of the Rating and Valuation Act, 1925. 224 H. C. Deb. 5 s. 978-9.

[48] 224 H. C. Deb. 5 s. 976 *et seq.*

[49] 72 H. L. Deb. 5 s. 1062.

[50] 256 H. C. Deb. 5 s. 637; 257 H. C. Deb. 5 s. 1012.

[51] E. g. 30 H. C. Deb. 5 s. 2007; 2013-4; 163 H. C. Deb. 5 s. 2106.

[52] 224 H. C. Deb. 5 s. 980.

[53] 98 *Hansard*, 3 s. 712; 224 H. C. Deb. 5 s. 984; 998; 225 H. C. Deb. 612.

The commonest argument in justification of delegated legislation advanced in Parliament was the fact that the authorities in whom legislative powers were proposed to be invested were, directly or indirectly, responsible to the House of Commons. The Ministers were of course responsible to the House; the permanent officials in the departments were responsible to the Ministers. Local authorities, School Boards, Trade Boards, Poor Law Commissioners, and the thousand and one executive agencies were either appointed by the Ministers or else subject to their supervision. All of them, thus, were directly or indirectly subject to the control of the House of Commons; consequently the theory of ministerial responsibility formed one of the strongest arguments at the disposal of the apologists of delegated legislation—an argument which they have exploited to the fullest extent.

Lord Althorp justified the investment of "extraordinary powers" in the Board of Poor Law Commissioners by the Poor Law Act, 1834, because "that power would be subject to the constant control of the Parliament and the Executive Government."[54] The School Commissioners in whom the Endowed Schools Act, 1869, proposed to vest discretionary powers "were but the creatures of the Government of the day, who would be responsible to Parliament for their proceedings, and that . . . would be sufficient to prevent any abuse of their powers."[55] The delegation of powers in the Local Government Act, 1888, was not an abnegation of the powers of Parliament because "the House must trust the Government of the day and its wisdom and its propositions."[56] The Rules of the House in 1894 would enable

[54] 22 *Hansard*, 3 s. 881.

[55] 194 *Hansard*, 3 s. 1411. *Cf.* also 196 *Hansard*, 3 s. 1747 for the remarks of Mr. Gladstone.

[56] Mr. Halley Stewart in 327 *Hansard*, 3 s. 640.

the House to keep a vigilant supervision over the exercise of the powers proposed to be delegated by the Local Government Act, 1894.[57] Though powers were granted to the Home Secretary by the Prison Act, 1898, "the House of Commons will hold the Home Secretary responsible for all the details of prison management." [58] Clause 1 of the Factory and Workshops Acts Amendment Act, 1901, was satisfactory to Sir Charles Dilke because "the whole responsibility will rest upon" the Home Secretary.[59] The Housing Act, 1909, would not lead to abuse of power because those who exercised these powers were responsible to the House of Commons.[60] "After all", contended Mr. MacCallum Scott, "the Government which exercises the power granted by the Defense of the Realm Act . . . is not an autocratic or oligarchic Government. It is still a Government responsible to this House, and unable to carry on without the continued support of this House." [61] The same gentleman,

[57] "The President of that Department", said the Earl of Winchilsea in the House of Lords, "was directly responsible to Parliament; his decisions could be challenged in various ways, and as much publicity would be given to them as if they were the decisions of Parliament. Questions might be put to him which he would be bound to answer, or his action might be challenged by a Vote on the Estimates to reduce his salary, or a private Member might put down a Motion in reference to his procedure. The challenge might be made as effective upon any decision the Local Government Board was likely to give, as could be the case in an appeal to Parliament." 21 *Hansard*, 4 s. 240.

[58] 60 *Hansard*, 4 s. 471.

[59] 95 *Hansard*, 4 s. 116.

[60] "After all", the Earl of Crewe said, "when noble Lords opposite talk about the advance of bureaucracy and the encroaching powers of Departments, at any rate those Departments are responsible to Parliament, and the Minister who is in charge can be called to account in either House by question or debate, and if his action is so desperately bad as to deserve public censure, he may in the last resort lose his office, or the Government of which he is a member may be removed from power." 3 H. L. Deb. 5 s. 1018.

[61] 70 H. C. Deb. 5 s. 330.

in the debate on the Emergency Powers Act, 1920, dismissed the charges of the Opposition by saying that there was an effective check upon the Government.[62] Mr. Gosling, the Minister of Transport, announced that for "every action taken" by the Minister with regard to London traffic, "the Minister will be responsible to Parliament."[63] A speech of similar purport was made by Mr. Sidney Webb, then President of the Board of Trade.[64]

In theory, all these propositions seem self-evident. In practice, however, the story is different. As shown in a preceding chapter, many members were fully aware that the Rules of the House give only a sporting chance to the private members to register their protests against any regulation which the Ministers lay on the Tables of the Houses. They also realized that a Government do not generally resign when they were defeated on a minor issue. As Mr. Herbert Morrison said, there were "times when Ministers were only nominally responsible to Parliament" during which Parliament had "no real control" over the Ministers at all.[65] The theory of ministerial responsibility, therefore, might sound infallible but it often failed to satisfy those who hoped to find in it an unfailing guarantee against ministerial encroachments.

The apologists have also endeavored to justify their position by showing that the actual exercise of legislative powers by the several authorities to whom they were transferred has so far not been characterized by abuses. If this demonstration is successful it is likely to prove extremely weighty and conclusions based upon it difficult to refute although the contention of executive infallibility was but infrequently

[62] 133 H. C. Deb. 5 s. 1647.

[63] 171 H. C. Deb. 5 s. 1701.

[64] 171 H. C. Deb. 5 s. 1779; see also 175 H. C. Deb. 5 s. 281.

[65] 171 H. C. Deb. 5 s. 1741.

advanced. The only counter-argument must of course be that the clean record of the past affords no assurance of similar performance in the future. Ministries changed. The conservative elements looked with abhorrence to a future when a Socialist Government should be in the saddle of government; the Socialists stood in equal fear of the possession of extensive powers by the Conservatives. But, as a weapon of defense, the argument is most valuable and a Minister's challenge to the Opposition to give instances of the misuse of previously delegated powers often leaves his critics silent.

Mr. Ritchie, in 1888, could announce "that in recent years, at any rate, the powers which had been wielded by Government Departments had been exercised wisely and to the public advantage." [66] Listing a series of Acts under the administration of the Local Government Board "over which he had the honour to preside", the Right Honourable Gentleman found that they were carried out admirably by "a Staff of great experience." [67] According to Major Astor, the experience with the administration of the Trade Boards Act, 1909, had been so satisfactory that the Minister should be given broad powers circumscribed by general principles enacted by Parliament.[68] Mr. Neville Chamberlain answered the charges of Sir Henry Slesser on Clause 130 of the Local Government Act, 1929, by saying that Sir Henry "has not been able to find a single instance . . . where Parliament has thought it necessary to raise the slightest shadow of complaint" and that "until he [Slesser] can show that this Clause has really brought about the sort of abuses which he has suggested, there is the thinnest

[66] 327 *Hansard*, 3 s. 633.

[67] 327 *Hansard*, 3 s. 998.

[68] 107 H. C. Deb. 5 s. 97.

sort of defense for his observations." [69] Inasmuch as the facts could not be disputed in this particular case, the appeal to the past record was an effective one. However, on an earlier occasion when Mr. John Burns attempted the same thing, he was answered by Sir Frederick Banbury in these words: [70]

I hope the right hon. Gentleman will not appeal if he wishes to influence me to anything that the present Government have done. I consider everything they have done is wrong. I do not remember them ever having done one right thing.

When reasoned argumentation yielded to such partisan spirit, any attempt to justify delegation by appealing to the past record could only result in failure; the Division Lobbies are thus the ultimate arbiter and the vote is the final test.

Sometimes the arguments used by the members of the Government in justification of delegated legislation consist in denials and contradictions of the facts and opinions of the critics. Most of these arguments were sheer expressions of personal preferences, difficult to prove and yet difficult to refute. The all-important consideration here was the angle from which the problem was approached and, though quite convincing sometimes, the debate really led nowhere.

Chief among these arguments was the discussion regarding the adequacy of the divers forms of safeguards that

[69] 224 H. C. Deb. 5 s. 976-7. Mr. Chamberlain continued: "I can confidently say that there has never arisen a case, where a Clause of this kind has had to be put into operation, where Parliament has found any reason to complain of the Minister who put it into operation." 224 H. C. Deb. 5 s. 980. This statement is borne out by the fact that of the Orders issued under the nine Acts which contain the Henry VIII Clause, "not one of them has ever been annulled by Parliament, before whom they have all been laid as soon as might be after having been made." Sir Hugh Orange, "Legislation by Whitehall", *Nineteenth Century*, June, 1932.

[70] 10 H. C. Deb. 5 s. 77-8 (Housing, Town Planning, etc. Act, 1909).

were embodied in the Bills presented. We have seen in the previous chapter that members made frequent demands for improving the safeguards to assure parliamentary control and to insure against ministerial abuse. In their speeches in support of this contention, they very naturally criticized the proposed safeguards as being inadequate. The apologists had to meet these criticisms by proving, to their own satisfaction at least, that the safeguards embodied in the Bills were adequate and would achieve their twofold purpose. Almost every Bill delegating legislative powers with safeguards was contested along these lines. To enumerate every instance would not only be impossible but profitless.[71]

[71] A few interesting examples, however, may be cited. The proposal that Rules issued under the Prison Act, 1898, should lie on the Table of both Houses for thirty days was said to "empower this House to keep a persistent and vigilant supervision over prison administration" because it was such "an excellent and perfectly sufficient safeguard." 56 *Hansard*, 4 s. 77-8 and 63 *Hansard*, 4 s. 412. Similarly, the safeguard of forty days on the Table of the House as provided in the Trade Boards Act, 1918, "is an ample safeguard." 107 H. C. Deb. 5 s. 64. Even the Emergency Powers Act, 1920, was said to be so "hedged round with safeguards of every kind that it would be practically impossible for any Government to abuse those powers." 42 H. C. Deb. 5 s. 103. The safeguard in the Rating and Valuation Act, 1925, "preserves the right of both Houses of Parliament." 188 H. C. Deb. 5 s. 1900. The safeguard in the Board of Guardians Act, 1926, "is quite sufficient for anyone" because the Minister could be held to account in case he exceeded or misused his powers, "and the Order made . . . would be rescinded by Order in Council." 197 H. C. Deb. 5 s. 2302-3. The procedure provided in the Local Government Act, 1929, assured, according to Sir H. Cautley, "a complete control over the Minister" and "therefore, the liberty of the subject is very well guarded." 224 H. C. Deb. 5 s. 988. Referring to the Board of Guardians Act, 1926, Sir Kingsley Wood declared in this debate that "Orders made by the Minister under that particular Act have been challenged again and again" so that "the Order under this Bill can be challenged in just the same way." 225 H. C. Deb. 5 s. 288. [According to Sir Arthur Robinson and Mr. E. J. Maude, representatives of the Ministry of Health before the Committee on Ministers' Powers, seventeen Orders were made by the Ministry of Health

In addition to proving the proposed safeguards adequate for their twofold purpose, apologists for delegated legislation frequently branded any proposal for more stringent safeguards as "unworkable", "unnecessary" or "impracticable".[72] Reasons were seldom given to support these assertions but the refusal of the Government to accept amendments providing for these more stringent safeguards

under the authority of the Board of Guardians Act, 1926, and on ten occasions a motion for an address was made. *Committee on Ministers' Powers: Minutes of Evidence*, vol. ii, p. 123]. Sir Thomas Inskip, the Attorney-General, summed up the whole argument in these words: "Whenever there is a provision put into a Bill ... that Parliament shall have an opportunity of approving and disapproving an Order, hon. Members opposite are very fond of telling us that that means nothing, because Parliament is quite certain to do what Ministers propose. Yet, on the other hand, supposing Ministers take power to do something without coming to Parliament, hon. Members say 'How monstrous that they should do something without asking Parliament to approve it.' It really passes my understanding why hon. Members who profess to believe so much in the interests of democracy and the particular expression of democracy which this House represents, can be so contemptuous of the decision of Parliament as to the wisdom or otherwise of an Order which is laid before Parliament. I believe it is a safeguard which all parties in the House recognise and value that Ministerial Orders should be submitted to Parliament for affirmation or rejection.... I venture to think that hon. Members opposite will find that every possible avenue is open to them and that, whether they come into office or remain on that side of the House, Parliament will have an opportunity of considering it." 225 H. C. Deb. 5 s. 300-2. *Cf.* also Sir Thomas's speech in 226 H. C. Deb. 5 s. 2511-7.

[72] Thus the proposal that the by-laws issued under the Municipal Corporations Act, 1882, should be approved by the Privy Council before they took effect was regarded as "unnecessary" by the Government. 269 *Hansard*, 3 s. 209-210. The amendment which would require all orders issued under the London Traffic Act, 1924, to be approved by resolution in the House of Commons was described as "much too complicated" and "positively mischievous" but was adopted by the House. 175 H. C. Deb. 5 s. 385. In 1926 a like proposal was made to the Board of Guardians Act, a proposal which Mr. Neville Chamberlain refused to sanction because it was "practically unworkable." 197 H. C. Deb. 5 s. 2441.

was usually sufficient to defeat the amendments if they were pressed to a division.

We have mentioned previously the resentment displayed by the critics of delegated legislation at the bureaucratic encroachments of the Government departments which, they thought, might lead to a dictatorship; in other words, " the new despotism " of Whitehall. In reply it was said that the safeguards provided were adequate to insure parliamentary control. One Minister, in 1834, ridiculed the idea by confessing that " it was the first time in his life that he heard anything denominated despotism which was subject to [parliamentary] control." [73] Ministers also paid high tribute to their subordinates whose integrity was beyond question or doubt.[74]

Very little was said in Parliament on the question of the judicial safeguard. Much, however, was said on the cognate subject of delegation of judicial or quasi-judicial powers. Many members, especially Ministers, believed that the ouster of the jurisdiction of the courts of law to declare regulations issued by the executive null and void on the ground of *ultra vires* was fully justified by modern circumstances. For one thing, it was believed that the numerous litigations expected to arise under the large numbers of regulations now being issued from Whitehall would so tax the resources of the courts as to be an impediment to their normal business. " It would be hopeless ", one member said, " to have appeals to the Courts of Law upon any of the questions arising under the " Education Act, 1902.[75] The complicated and technical nature of these regulations, moreover, would often find the courts lacking in the aptitude to pass judgment upon them. " The idea of the Bill ", said

[73] 23 *Hansard*, 3 s. 985. *Cf.* also 25 *Hansard*, 3 s. 984.

[74] 20 *Hansard*, 4 s. 1098. *Cf.* also 272 *Hansard*, 3 s. 589.

[75] 113 *Hansard*, 4 s. 1239.

Mr. Lloyd George on the Patents and Designs Act, 1907, " was that there should be a special Judge with special knowledge of patent cases who should sit upon patent business." [76] Furthermore, the judicial process, it was said, " is a process slow, cumbrous, and costly." [77] It meant red-tape and great delay.[78] In the end, the original intentions of the Government to achieve efficiency and despatch might be defeated. The Government departments did not suffer from these defects and they were the proper places for appeal. Finally, the temper of the courts was as a rule conservative. " When they interpret " a statute, " it is not often according to the wants of this age, but according to the letter in which these wants were defined at the time of the foundation." [79] These are reasons for the delegation of judicial or quasi-judicial powers but they can be employed to justify the ousting of the power of independent scrutiny of the courts over certain classes of regulations which such delegation necessarily entails.

In conclusion it is interesting to note that in the earlier days the justification of the proposed grant usually came before any attack was made. Ministers introducing a Bill for First Reading or Second Reading often indulged in long speeches in support of their demands for legislative powers. Now, however, they have ceased to be so apologetic. They usually await the attacks of the Opposition and reply just before the Division so that the Opposition may not have a chance of rebuttal. In other words, as delegated legislation came to be the "common form of legislation", the Government relied increasingly upon the ties of party for success.

[76] 180 *Hansard*, 4 s. 1186. The Clause which provided for appeal to the Comptroller was, after vehement opposition, taken out of the Bill.

[77] 194 *Hansard*, 3 s. 1369 (Endowed Schools Act, 1869).

[78] *Cf.* Mr. John Burns's remarks in 10 H. C. Deb. 5 s. 238-9.

[79] 194 *Hansard*, 3 s. 1369.

CHAPTER VI

Conclusion

In the preceding pages we have analysed the criticisms, remedies and justification of delegated legislation expressed and suggested by members of Parliament when Bills delegating legislative powers to the Privy Council, the Government departments and the other executive authorities were being considered. This analysis of parliamentary opinion is prefaced by a brief résumé of the opinion of what Professor Maitland calls "the institutional writers". It is seen that an overwhelming majority of them agree that delegated legislation, being "a concomitant of modern legislation", is an inevitable tendency. Some writers believe that much can be said in its favor while others think that it has gone far beyond its reasonable limits. The abolition of the practice root and branch, though desired by some, is never seriously advocated. Proposals for improvements are profuse and they usually aim at the betterment of the safeguards, administrative, parliamentary and judicial.

Our sketch of the history of parliamentary opinion of delegated legislation shows that Parliament has become increasingly alarmed as more and more Bills delegating legislative powers have been presented by successive Governments. But, unfortunately, this awakening is belated, for it comes after party fealty has considerably lessened the significance of parliamentary debate. Parliamentary criticisms of delegated legislation, however, increase in vigor and loquacity. Heroics are freely indulged in and devices are suggested to arrest the menacing growth of delegated legislation. This mounting avalanche of criticisms, the Ministers and their aides meet with equal force. Taken as a whole, it has been the intention in these chapters to present a more or less digested picture of an important section of British opinion on a method of law-making rapidly becoming fashionable at the expense of age old methods and traditions. Parliamentary debate may be a travesty, "a nuisance", but the British government being a democratic system, the continued manifestation of a trend of public opinion may prove an invaluable warning to those who are in the saddle.

Delegated legislation, not being a party issue as such, is often the subject of candid and occasionally non-partisan criticism. Parliamentary critics find that it has done irreparable damage to that rare flower of British political genius—the English Constitution—which breathes, among other theories, the venerable "ancient liberties", the separation of powers, parliamentary sovereignty, and the principle of democracy itself. Delegated legislation, moreover, is said to have so exalted the powers of the executive branch of government that these powers can easily be exercised autocratically and despotically. Furthermore, the increase of the powers of the executive means the increase of the powers of the civil service which may come to possess all the vices of a "bureaucracy" in the true continental sense of the term. To vindicate the constitution, to forestall a would-be dictatorship of the Cabinet, and to prevent the establishment of a "bureaucracy" in England, Parliament should strive hard to retain, or to regain, its control through safeguards so framed that they will not only provide immediate redress when delegated powers are abused but insure against abuse as well.

Confronted by such weighty arguments, the apologists of delegated legislation are not entirely helpless. Occasionally, out of a twinge of conscience perhaps, the Ministers and their aides bring in an amendment or two mitigating part of their original demands for discretionary rule-making powers. More often, they meet their adversaries on their own ground with logic which to partisan ears must appear remorseless and which fails to stir only the graceless hearts of the Opposition. They refer to the needs of a rapidly changing age to prove that the old bottle of established constitutional doctrines will no longer hold the new wine of altered circumstances. Parliament, they say, is hopelessly congested; the intricacies of modern government demand more elasticity in its laws; national crises can only be averted with efficiency and despatch. Past Governments have obtained similar powers from Parliament; those who exercise these powers are responsible to the House of Commons; there is on record no abuse of delegated powers. The safeguards provided are ample and adequate to insure parliamentary control; the courts can always pronounce a regulation null and void on the ground of *ultra vires;* the Ministers, members of Parliament themselves, love the constitution; they have no intention to install a dictatorship of the Cabinet; the civil service is still the best in the world and is free from the vices of a " bureaucracy ".

Thus, the battle is joined. But delegated legislation, the child of changing needs, continues to grow vigorously. The violence and persistency of attack may circumscribe its dimensions at times, but a return to " the legislative monopoly " of Parliament is something to which only the most unreasonable still aspire.

Again, Governments come and go. The critics of today are the champions of to-morrow. Lord Hewart, a hard-biting opponent of delegated legislation, has to defend measures delegating extensive legislative powers before the House of Commons because these measures happen to be sponsored by his own party. The " watchdogs of the constitution " are found in the rank and file of every party. Their enthusiasm often depends upon the side of the gangway where they chance to sit. The moment the Whips crack, desire to defend the constitution yields to the still stronger desire to remain " a loyal son ". Defender or no defender, members walk into the Lobby to which they belong.

BIBLIOGRAPHY

I. Primary Sources

Hansard Parliamentary Debates, 3rd ser., 1830-1891, 350 vols.

Hansard Parliamentary Debates, 4th ser., 1892-1908, 77 vols.

House of Commons Debates (H. C. Deb.), 5th ser., 1909 to date.

House of Lords Debates (H. L. Deb.), 5th ser., 1909 to date.

Journal of the House of Commons, issued each session since 1547.

The Statutory Rules and Orders Revised, 1896, 1st ed., 8 vols., containing such Statutory Rules and Orders of a Public General Character issued before 1890 as were then in force.

Statutory Rules and Orders, issued annually since 1890, edited by Alexander Pulling, 1890-1922, by C. T. Carr, 1922—.

The Statutory Rules and Orders Revised 1904, 13 vols., containing all Statutory Rules and Orders of a Public General character as were then in force, edited by Alexander Pulling.

Manuals of Emergency Legislation:

(1) Containing all Rules and Orders up to September 30, 1914, edited by Alexander Pulling.

(2) Supplement to (1), edited by Alexander Pulling.

(3) Financial Edition, up to June 4, 1915, edited by Alexander Pulling.

(4) Defense of the Realm Edition, 7th ed., revised up to March 31, 1919, edited by Sir Charles Cook.

(5) Food Supply Manual, 1st ed., revised up to May 15, 1917, edited by Alexander Pulling.

(6) Food (Supply and Production) Manual, 1st enlarged edition, superseding edition of 1917, revised up to October 21, 1917, edited by Alexander Pulling.

Parliamentary Papers, Accounts and Papers, containing weekly list of Statutory Rules and Orders lying on the Table of the House of Commons, not circulated to individual members but may be obtained at the Vote Office.

Chitty's Statutes of Practical Utility, 1235 to date, edited by Joseph Chitty and later by W. H. Aggs, containing also selected Statutory Rules.

Report of the Committee on Ministers' Powers, Cmd. 4060/1932.

Memoranda Submitted to and Evidence Taken before the Committee on Ministers' Powers, 2 vols., 1932.

Parliamentary Papers, Report of the Select Committee on Procedure, 1914.

Parliamentary Papers, Special Report from the Select Committee on Public Business, no. 161, 1931, only evidence published.

II. Secondary Sources

1. books

Allen, C. K., *Law in the Making*, 2nd ed., revised and enlarged, Oxford, 1930.

——, *Bureaucracy Triumphant*, London, 1931, a collection of articles written by Professor Allen.

Anson, Sir William, *Law and Custom of the Constitution*, vol. i, Gwyer ed., London, 1922.

Carr, Cecil T., *Delegated Legislation*, Cambridge, 1921.

Chiao, Wan Hsuan, *Devolution in Great Britain*, New York, 1926.

Comer, John P., *Legislative Functions of National Administrative Authorities*, New York, 1927.

Dicey, A. V., *Law of the Constitution*, 8th ed., London, 1915.

——, *Lectures on the Relation between Law and Public Opinion in England During the Nineteenth Century*, London, 1914.

Duguit, Leon, *Law in the Modern State*, English translation by Frida and Harold J. Laski, New York, 1919.

Fairlie, John A., *Administrative Procedure in Connection with Statutory Rules and Orders in Great Britain*, Urbana, 1927.

——, *British War Administration*, Carnegie Endowment for International Peace, 1922.

Finer, Herman, *The Theory and Practice of Modern Government*, 2 vols., London, 1932.

Hewart, Lord Chief Justice, *The New Despotism*, New York, 1929.

——, *Essays and Observations*, London, 1930.

Ilbert, Sir Courtenay, *Legislative Methods and Forms*, London, 1901.

——, *Methods of Legislation*, London, 1912.

——, *The Mechanics of Law-Making*, New York, 1914.

Keith, Arthur B., *An Introduction to British Constitutional Law*, Oxford, 1931.

Keir, D. L. and Lawson, F. H., *Cases in Constitutional Law*, Oxford, 1928.

Laski, Harold J., *A Grammar of Politics*, London, 1925.

——, *Authority in the Modern State*, New Haven, 1919.

——, *Foundations of Sovereignty*, New Haven, 1921.

——, *Democracy in Crisis*, North Carolina, 1933.

Lees-Smith, H. B., *A Guide to Parliamentary and Official Papers*, Oxford, 1924.

Low, Sir Sidney, *The Governance of England*, 2nd ed., New York, 1922.
Lowell, A. Lawrence, *The Government of England*, 2nd ed., 2 vols., New York, 1916.
MacBain, Howard L. and Rogers, Lindsay, *New Constitutions of Europe*, New York, 1922.
MacIlwain, Charles H., *The High Court of Parliament and Its Supremacy*, New Haven, 1910.
Maitland, F. W., *Constitutional History of England*, London, 1920.
Muir, Ramsay, *Peers and Bureaucrats*, London, 1910.
——, *How Britain is Governed*, New York, 1930.
Marriott, J. A. R., *Mechanism of the Modern State*, London, 1927, 2 vols.
——, *English Political Institutions*, Oxford, 1925.
——, *The Crisis of English Liberty*, New York, 1930.
Ogg, Frederick Austin, *English Government and Politics*, New York, 1928.
Port, F. J., *Administrative Law*, London, 1929.
Redlich, Josef, *History of the Procedure of the House of Commons*, 3 vols., London, 1908.
Robson, William A., *Justice and Administrative Law*, London, 1928.
Thring, Lord, *Practical Legislation*, London, 1902.
Todd, Alpheus, *On Parliamentary Government in England*, 2 vols., 1st ed., 1867, 2nd ed., 1887, London.
Troup, Sir Edward, *The Home Office*, London, 1925.
Wade, E. C. S. and Phillips, Godfrey, *Constitutional Law*, London, 1931.
Willoughby, W. W. and Rogers, Lindsay, *An Introduction to the Problem of Government*, New York, 1921.

II. ARTICLES

Allen, C. K., "Some Aspects of Administrative Law", *Journal of the Society of Public Teachers of Law*, 1929.
Bontecou, Eleanor, "Delegation of Powers", *Encyclopedia of Social Science*, vol. v.
Bowman, Harold M., "Martial Law and the English Constitution", *Michigan Law Review*, December, 1916.
Chalmers, M. D., "The English Statute Book", *Edinburgh Review*, April, 1924.
Clarke, Sidney W., "The Rule of Dora", *Journal of Comparative Legislation and International Law*, vol. i, 3rd ser. (1919).
Dicey, A. V., "The Development of Administrative Law in England", *Law Quarterly Review*, April, 1915.
Elliott, Frank, "More Bureaucracy", *Cornhill Magazine*, September, 1932.
Finer, Herman, "Special Report from the Select Committee on Procedure on Public Business", *Political Quarterly*, July-September, 1932, a review.

Gaus, John M., "The Report of the British Committee on Ministers' Powers", *American Political Science Review*, December, 1932.

Gibbon, I. G., Gwyer, M. L. and Anderson, Paul, "The Powers of Public Departments to Make Rules Having the Force of Law", *Public Administration*, 1927.

Henderson, J. S. and Laski, Harold J., "A Note on Parliamentary Time and the Problem of Devolution", *Economica*, March, 1925.

Hopkins, Sir Richard V. N., "The Expert and the Layman", *Public Administration*, 1925.

Ilbert, Sir Courtenay, "A Review of Carr", *Delegated Legislation, Journal of Comparative Legislation and International Law*, 1922.

Jennings, W. Ivor, "The Constitution under Strain", *Political Quarterly*, April-June, 1932.

——, A Review of the *Report of the Committee on Ministers' Powers, Public Administration*, October, 1932.

Laing, B. M. and Gwyer, M. L., "The Legislative Functions of Government Departments", *Public Administration*, 1930.

Laski, Harold J., "The Mother of Parliaments", *Foreign Affairs*, July, 1931.

——, "The Growth of Administrative Discretion", *Public Administration*, 1923.

——, "The British Crisis of 1931", *Political Quarterly*, October-December, 1931.

——, "The Limitations of the Expert", *Harpers Magazine*, December, 1930.

——, "Bureaucracy", *Encyclopedia of Social Science*, vol. iii.

Lees-Smith, H. B., "The Timetable of the House of Commons", *Economica*, June, 1924.

Macassey, Sir Lynden, "Law-Making by Government Departments", *Journal of Comparative Legislation and International Law*, 1923.

Marriott, J. A. R., "Law and Liberty", *Fortnightly Review*, July, 1928.

——, "Liberty and Law", *Edinburgh Review*, October, 1929.

——, "Whitehall and Westminster", *Edinburgh Review*, January, 1926.

——, "English Constitution in Transition", *Quarterly Review*, January, 1925, reprinted as introduction to his *English Political Institutions*.

Orange, Sir Hugh, "Legislation by Whitehall", *Nineteenth Century*, June, 1932.

Pollock, James K., Jr., "The Position of the British Parliament", *American Political Science Review*, August, 1931.

Potter, Harold, "Legislative Powers of Public Authorities", *Public Administration*, January, 1928.

Rogers, Lindsay, "The War and the English Constitution", *The Forum*, July, 1915.

——, "Parliamentary Commissions in France", *Political Science Quarterly*, September and December, 1923.

Robson, William A., "A Charge of Despotism", *Contemporary Review*, January, 1930, a review of Hewart's *The New Despotism*.

——, "The Report of the Committee on Ministers' Powers", *Political Quarterly*, July-September, 1932.

Rosenbaum, Samuel, "Rule-Making in the Courts of the Empire", *Journal of Comparative Legislation and International Law*, 1915.

Schuyler, Robert L., A Review of Marriott's "The Crisis of English Liberty", *Political Science Quarterly*, June, 1931.

——, "The Decline of the House of Commons", *Columbia University Quarterly*, October, 1919.

Smellie, K. B., "Some Aspects of English Administrative Law", *Public Administration*, 1927.

Scott, Sir Leslie, "The Rule of Law in Present Constitutional Practice", *Contemporary Review*, May, 1931.

Stamp, Sir Josiah, "Recent Tendencies Towards the Devolution of Legislative Functions to the Administration", *Public Administration*, 1924.

Suzman, Arthur, "Administrative Law in England: A Study of the Report of the Committee on Ministers' Powers", *Iowa Law Review*, January, 1933.

Taylor, G. R. Sterling, "Government by Amateurs", *Nineteenth Century*, May, 1928.

Webb, Mrs. Sidney, "A Reform Bill for 1932", *Political Quarterly*, January-March, 1931.

Willis, John, "The Delegation of Legislative and Judicial Powers to Administrative Bodies: A Study of the Report of the Committee on Ministers' Powers", *Iowa Law Review*, January, 1933.

Young, E. Hilton, "The Authority of the House of Commons", *Contemporary Review*, July, 1925.

III. NEWSPAPERS

London Times, March 4, 1911; February 16, 1929.

Manchester Guardian, weekly edition, February 1, 1929.

New York Times, "Expound to Britain Her Constitution", July 20, 1932.

INDEX

Bei Fragen zur Produktsicherheit wenden Sie sich bitte an:
If you have any questions regarding product safety,
please contact:

Walter de Gruyter GmbH
Genthiner Straße 13
10785 Berlin
productsafety@degruyterbrill.com